Diagnose and Repair

Thought-Provoking and Mentally Inspiring

DR. LYNN EARL KIRKLAND

ISBN: 978-1-6847-0718-8 (sc)
ISBN: 978-1-6847-0717-1 (e)

Library of Congress Control Number: 2019908884

Lulu Publishing Services rev. date: 07/10/2019

Dedication

I want to dedicate this source of help to the many people across this world who are living in pain associated with memories from their past. I dedicate this message in this book to the individual that sits alone in silence thinking and contemplating suicide. I dedicate this work to the many people that have been searching for years for answers to UN answered questions. This work is dedicated to the children who had a parent absent from their lives and to the absent parent. Too often opportunities for great relations ships to exist between an absent parents with their child is blocked by his or her on thoughts are Ideas.

This work is dedicated to the child who was poisoned by one parent to dislike the other parent. This book contents and labor of this book is dedicated to the individuals who are good at providing new problems every time they hear a solution to a problem. This work is dedicated to the individuals who are great at building mental prisons for themselves. For those of you who are in ruts and can't seem to get out this work is dedicated to you. For the ones who thinks that they are always right and everyone else is wrong this work is dedicated to you. For the Individuals that are always listing to people to only respond and not listing for understanding or wisdom this work is for you.

I know that people are hurting all over this world for many reasons and that intervention at the right moment can change a life for the better and possible save a life. Therefore I dedicated this labor of love to all of humanity in hopes that Diagnose and Repair will be found by those who are looking and ready for a better way of life. To those who will refuse to forgive others this book is dedicated to you.

Finally this book is dedicated to helping a person get to the root cause of any personal problem with steps and solutions on how to resolve those problems. One of the understandings that life has taught me is that a problem can only exist when there is no solutions.

I have also heard that Knowledge is powerful therefore if what I have been searching for does not exist in my mind. It is time to go seeking elsewhere and be conscious of which knowledge is beneficial to you and which is harmful. I believe that Kenny Rogers said in a song something like this you got to know when to hold them, know when to fold them, know when to walk away and when to run. May you be one of the many who will be blessed by the contents of Diagnose and Repair?

Preface

As a minister of the gospel of Jesus, I have sometimes felt as though I am a magnet for people who are hurting emotionally. I mention this thought because during my forty-seven years of serving in ministry, I have met many people whom I did not know and they would share with me their problems. I have often had family members, church members, friends, associates, and strangers share with me the troubles that were causing them emotional pain.

What I have noticed from these conversations is there are commonalities in the dialogues. The things that they shared relating to their issues resided in the thoughts of the individuals and their understanding of what happened at specific moments in their lives. It seems to be a part of human nature to not see oneself clearly or take ownership of one's contribution to an issue that has happened and is still troubling the person mentally. The result of this is often conveyed in the delivery of their story.

Granted, I do understand that sometimes we are faced with troubles that we did nothing to provoke. When this occurs, it often takes time for a person to reach a level of maturity where the individual stops thinking of oneself as the victim. Also consider the mental state and condition of the person or people who caused the lasting mental pain. To view a moment in time in this way requires taking a close look at all involved, including your own choices and actions. This could very well provide much-needed answers as to why and how this happened to you. Second, the path to healing begins with a person's acceptance of his or her choices that led to a set of circumstances. Life's mental issues are not always caused by someone else. We are also contributors to many of our life's problems.

From the book of Proverbs, I have learned this to be true. "All a man's ways seem right to him, but the Lord weighs the heart" (Proverbs 21:2 NIV). I find it easy to be misled by my own thoughts, and I do not think I am alone.

I have shared with many people what I have learned through life via experiences, studying, and believing and practicing what the word of God teaches us. I know that practicing these principles has made a difference in my life and helped me to become a better person.

After many years of serving in the ministry of preaching, pastoring, counseling, and listening to so many sad stories from people, the Holy Spirit provided me help to understand the accumulation of information from those experiences. That understanding produced the wisdom that I relied on to help me with expanding on what I shared in my first similar publication of this book, as well as what I am compelled to share in this version.

What I have learned from studying the Bible has helped me tremendously, and I've shared what I've learned with others in an effort help them. This message that I have been blessed to compose can go where I cannot go and be where I cannot be. This is one of my contributions to the world to help those who are hurting and are troubled with the challenges of sifting through the many thoughts of their own minds.

Contents

Dedication v
Preface vii

1 The Gift and functioning of the Holy Spirit 1
2 Warnings & searching for personal UN answered questions 4
3 Dealing with our desires and get too the cause of an emotional problem 6
4 Lessons from Conversations 9
5 Examining some of the emotional issues that a child may have relating to parents 12
6 Male and female creation account, their sin and punishment 15
7 God's plan for mankind and learning to let go of weights 23
8 Purposely designed Information and Images of Jesus 27
9 Dangers ways of dealing with unnecessary burdens 30
10 Getting to and identifying the root cause of a problem 33
11 Focus on factual thoughts, prepare for Satan's attacks and be alert 40
12 Internal and external body parts and purposes 45
13 Walk in righteousness and God will provide for and protect you... 51
14 The Bible message and Jesus teachings 54
15 Processing knowledge and using discernment 57
16 The Avatar scene and the war within 60
17 Opening the door to allow Jesus requires an inside decisions 63
18 Steps to help the new believer to enter God's Kingdom 67
19 Biblical instructions to family members in God's kingdom 73

Conclusion 79
Thank you 81
About the Author 83

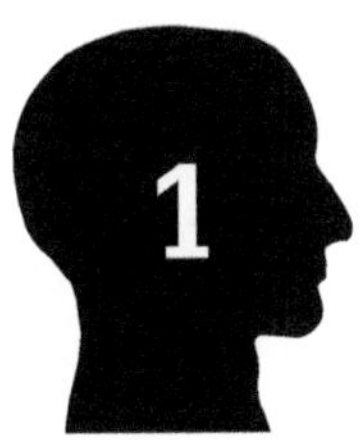

The Gift and functioning of the Holy Spirit

My Greatest Teacher

This book was first published in 2010 as *Learning and Understanding How to Manage Our Lives Effectively with the Battle That Exists Within.* Since then, I have grown in knowledge, understanding, wisdom, and spirituality. I also have had many more conversations that reminded me of conversations that I'd had with others in the past. I have had the opportunity to sit in the presence of a great teacher, and I have participated in Dr. Myles Munroe's mentoring program. I have received an honorary doctorate from Pater Theological Seminary in Abilene, Texas.

I have researched a great deal of literature, and I have arrived at this understanding that my greatest teacher has been with me ever since I accepted Jesus the Christ as my personal savior at the age of nine. My greatest teacher has been in the gift of the Holy Spirit—his presence and role in my life. Jesus told his disciples that he would not leave them alone and that the Counselor would come.

Jesus's Promise of the Holy Spirit

> If you love me, you will obey what I command. And I will ask the Father, and he will give you another Counselor to be with you forever—the Spirit of truth. The world cannot accept him, because it neither sees him nor knows him. But you know him, for he lives with you and will be in you. I will not leave you as orphans; I will come to you. (John 14:15–19 NIV)

The Spirit of Truth Will Be Our Guide

> I have much more to say to you, more than you can now bear. But when he, the Spirit of truth, comes, he will guide you into all truth. He will not speak on his own; he will speak only what he hears, and he will tell you what is yet to come. He will bring glory to me by taking from what is mine and making it known to you. All that belongs to the Father is mine. That is why I said the Spirit will take from what is mine and make it known to you. (John 16:12–15 NIV)

To receive this gift from God, you must believe in his son, Jesus, and live by faith, trusting in his teachings and obeying his words. It is his truth that will help any person with his or her thinking. The Bible teaches us in Philippians 2:5 that "Your attitude should be the same as that of Christ Jesus."

To let the mind of Christ be in you, you will need to read the synoptic Gospels and the writings of Paul in order to learn what was and is the mind of Christ Jesus. These texts are teachings that will become a part of our psyches once we become familiar with them. This knowledge is now a part of our thoughts and can be used to transform our old way of thinking and into a new one, which will provide for us a better way of making choices that leads to a better way of life.

Pray for Understanding and Guidance

I have prayed and asked God on many occasions to help me identify words to share with a person that could help him or her. I believe that the contents of this book are a major part of my answer.

I have asked God this because each individual is different, and he is omniscient. It is through him that I find the wisdom that is needed to help any person. God knows every individual's thoughts, deeds, past, present, and future, and he knows what he or she needs to hear to be helped. We know only what people reveal to us either by words or actions, but God knows what is in their minds and hearts. Whether those people take heed or not is totally up to them. Some people are very good at camouflaging themselves in their conversations and hiding the truth. When a person is truly seeking help you will not find it that way.

One time I preached a sermon Tiled "Don't be a Hard Knot". I had visited a friend of mine Marvin, who had a wood heater. While visiting with him I noticed in his yard a block of wood with a not on it and a metal wedge stuck in the block of wood. This piece of wood refused to be split and would not let go of the wedge. That piece of wood could have serve a purpose. I have found out that there are many people just like that hard block of wood.

Warnings & searching for personal UN answered questions

Sometimes I have been prompted to warn people to stop doing the thing that I knew they were doing, things that could cause them pain. I would reach out to them and share what I felt that I needed to share, and if they refused to heed my advice, the results ended up being calamitous. I knew that if they had taken heed of the warning, the results would have been totally different. I have felt sorrow and pain for those I have warned. I finally grew tired of hurting for people who continue on a path of destruction. An old saying came to my mind as a reminder that I can only share the advice and that's it. It is up to the recipient to use it: "You can lead a horse to water, but you can't make it drink." After preaching and dealing with people for so many years, I have learned the true meaning of that saying.

I need to be able to use words in a message or conversation that could cause a person to truly think about where the root cause of his or her problem resides. The problem is not within the body but within the mind of the soul. However, I have noticed in many of these conversations that these people were looking not for understanding but rather for a reply.

It is our thoughts that can cause us the greatest problems in life if we fail to truly evaluate the basis of those thoughts before acting on them. Wisdom has taught me that the hardest problems an individual may encounter in life are internal, not external. I remember watching shows like *Long Lost Family* in which people of many different ages have struggled for years to find relatives so they could ask those questions that they had been holding on to for years. Many of these individuals had allowed the questions to negatively interfere with their lives. If their parents were evil individuals who had committed horrific crimes, often they lived in fear of becoming like their parents. I understand that fear is created by our own thoughts. I remember reading some time ago that one definition of *fear* is "false expectations appearing as real."

I have watched the show *Long Island Medium*, where people turned to a medium in their search for answers from the deceased. You can spend a lifetime looking for an answer that does not exist, but the question can still linger in your mind. Learning to manage these thoughts and placing less value on them could change your emotions about needing an answer. Learning to live your life without an answer would get rid of the burden of needing an answer. If your question makes you miserable, there comes a point where you should realize that it is time to reset that thought and abandon the thinking. Move on with your life with a positive way of thinking. Life will get better.

Dealing with our desires and get too the cause of an emotional problem

The Desire Factor

All of us have the desire factor in common. We all share desires that are associated with our five senses: taste, sight, smell, hearing, and touch. Our senses trigger emotions, and emotions want to be satisfied. Once they are satisfied, the urge is no longer present.

Many of our desires are harmful, and this is where failure occurs. Failing to notice or ignoring the danger of satisfying a harmful desire is what will cause a person emotional suffering. The Holy Spirit is very capable of assisting any person with the control needed to avoid a potential desire disaster. Consider, for example, thirst and hunger. When a person desires water and then drinks water, the desire is satisfied. When a person desires to eat, that desire is satisfied when the persons eats. We all know that thirst and hunger can be quenched with different liquids or foods, but we also know that not all liquids and foods are healthy for us. Do we always eat and drink what is good for us?

It is very important to know which desires are beneficial to you. Let's examine what the apostle Paul had to say about what is beneficial. "'Everything is permissible'—but not everything is beneficial. 'Everything is permissible'—but not everything is constructive. Nobody should seek his own good, but the good of others" (1 Corinthians 10:23–24). To get the best out of our lives, we can learn from the teachings of Paul and others that not everything we think of doing is beneficial. My own experience and observations have taught me that failure to honor godly principles and laws can cause a person to experience much unwanted and unnecessary pain.

The reason I ask God to give me the words or message for my audience is that he knows the individuals. After many of my sermons, I have received confirmation from congregants struggling with thoughts and problems that the message that I had preached on that day was for him or her. It was not my intentions to prepare a message for a specific individual whom I knew or didn't know. I never know who will be present to hear a sermon or lesson, but God does, and I love how he places us in the right place at the right time. This would not have happened if it were not for the assistance of the Holy Spirit, provided by an all-knowing and wise God.

I have also had people who have come to me upset or have left the church because they felt that either parts or all of the message that I had delivered on that day was about them. Some people who had become members where I was an under shepherd have told me that their reason for leaving the church they had been attending was that they had told the pastor something in private and then heard it in a sermon later.

It is a common thing for humans to have many of the same issues. My advice is if you hear a message from a pastor or preacher that sounds familiar, as though he or she is talking about you or to you, then you should listen for the beneficial information in it.

While I am studding and preparing a message, I need my ears to be open to the Holy Spirit—and I am not referring to the two attached to my head. I want to hear what God has to say because the people are God's people. It is the same for me with counseling: I need my spiritual ears to hear what the Holy Spirit is saying to me.

The problems that I am referring to and focusing on are not physically related. However, physical ailments can cause some mental stress and emotional turbulence.

In almost all of the conversations that I've had with individuals concerning the problems that they were dealing with in the present, those problems had been layered over time from his or her thoughts concerning a matter. One way of describing these layers for imagination is that of an onion. An onion has many layers surrounding the core, and in order to expose the core, you will have to remove each outer layer. I do not find this task to be easy because once the skin of the onion is broken, the aroma that provides flavor will also cause my eyes to water. Even with burning eyes, I continue peeling and cutting because I know the flavor of that eye burning onion will give me what I want in what I am about to cook.

In the same way, it will not be easy peeling back the layers of our memories that are tangled up in many thoughts. Each layer needs to be examined through the lens of truth, meaning that you will examine not only others' choices, actions, and behaviors but also your own choices, actions, and behaviors. This must be done to eliminate false perceptions to understand the truth about the matter. The truth will provide a much better way of thinking, which will transform your life for the better.

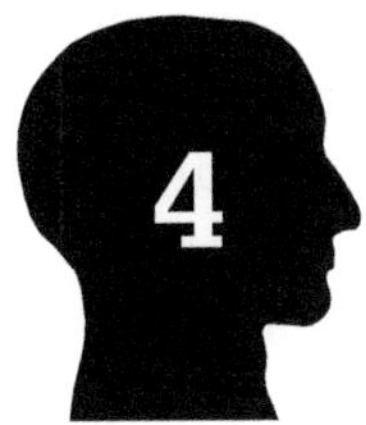

Lessons from Conversations

There are many times in our lives that we do not possess the power to change things and the people around us, but with God's help, we can learn to think different about those things.

There are many thoughts people are struggling with that are related to something that has happened in their lives, whether long ago or in the recent past. The things that were troubling them were buried deep inside under layers of time.

These individuals have had numerous conversations with themselves and others about these same troubling issues. I have come to the understanding that these conclusions are quite often self-related to their thinking and interpretations of the matter.

In many instances, some of the mental healing could have been easily done by simply forgiving the people who had caused pain, or by simply owning one's choices and actions. Sometimes the answer to a problem can be found in good advice. However, when a person is listening only to respond and not for understanding, he or she will miss the value in what was said.

I have noticed in many of these conversations that the people never took responsibility for their actions when others were involved. This caused them to blame everyone else about what had happened, not themselves. The failure to acknowledge your contributions to and participation in a problem establishes a false sense of innocence. It is also a natural thing for a person to tell the facts concerning them and another person in which the former is the victim and the latter is the aggressor.

I have heard it said on many different occasions that there are two types of people in the world, givers and takers. I've learned that there are other kinds of people in the world as well. There are those who always are negative; even when they're trying to say something positive, they end up on a negative note. There are also those who think they are always right and everyone else is wrong.

There are those who, because of their education in a particular field of study, ignore or refuse to allow others to share their understanding of the matter being discussed. These individuals appear to portray the sense of not understanding what others are saying.

A good example of this is people who have been trained in a medical profession. They have been trained in such a way that many will not accept any outside treatment or help if they become ill.

People who are negative talkers in conversations are toxic and poisonous, and they do not perceive themselves as being negative or wrong. As I try to change the direction of these types of conversations, I can easily become a victim of the individual's negativity. I know this to be true because I've have experienced it on numerous occasions.

I've also tried on many different occasions to bring this information to an individual's attention. Upon my trying to share the information, it was often not received as helpful knowledge or wisdom from me.

The response from the individual becomes one of defense. Another very important thing that I've learned while trying to help people is that you can only help the ones who want to be helped. Some people have a problem for every solution that's given to them. When you provide them with a solution, they present you with a new problem.

In one of Dr. Myles Munroe's conferences, he told us, "Don't think that because you have learned all of this information, people will want to hear what you have to say." I have learned from that statement to listen for a question when I am having a conversation with a person who is in need of advice. I understand the question as an interest from the person regarding what I have to say.

Sometimes people with big egos will not allow themselves to receive what you're sharing. These individuals usually interrupt what you are saying to tell you what they have to say. If this behavior persists, you can abandon this conversation to spare your own frustrations with that conversation.

Some people simply want to tell you their stories. These individuals will interrupt your conversation while you are speaking and use up as much of your time as you are willing to allow. Here is where I began to question the motives of why they called me or why they wanted to talk to me, when in reality they would not allow me to say anything. It took me a long time to recognize this type of conversation and what was really happening.

I have found these conversations to be very stressful and time-consuming, and they usually leave me emotionally drained. In many of these conversations, I will say to an individual, "Okay, I have to go now." To me, it seems as though they never hear what I said because they never stop talking.

In the past, I have shared this information during a Bible class at our church. I have made copies and passed them out in an effort to help those present via what I had learned. It is my belief that what I have learned can help others, and I want to share this knowledge with the world. I pray that this book will be a blessing and help to people as they travel along this life's journey.

All of us have problems that we have gone through in life, and we will face many more if God allows us to continue to live. However, many have never been able to move forward from a particular moment in time that has caused some emotional wounds. It is my prayer that the contents of this book will provide insight on new ways of thinking and living. One of the things that were brought up as a personal problem in many of my conversations involved issues relating to parents.

Examining some of the emotional issues that a child may have relating to parents

Unresolved Parent Problems

One of the many conversations that I had with people identified their problems as being associated with parents. Either a parent was not present, or the people had a problem with how they were treated or raised by parents or guardians.

In the case of the absent parent, it seems as though people may have a preconceived fantasy of how their lives would have been with the absent parent present. Therefore the absent parent is blamed because the fantasy never happened.

In other words, the sons or daughters think their lives wouldn't be in the condition they are in if the absent parent had been present. This idea is mostly present in the minds of individuals who shared with me their stories and were not happy with their lives. It is as though in their minds, the absent parent's presence would had some magical power to make things better. Because he or she was absent, that person seemingly became the cause of all of the child's problems.

Here is a reality to consider: the entire idea of the absent parent's presence helping is only assumed. People really don't know if a parent's presence would have made things better or worse.

The other thing that can cause a child to become mentally messed up is the parent who is raising the child. There are parents who have poisoned their own children with their venom toward the absent parent. The child is taught in such a way that often he or she ends up with additional hatred toward the absent parent. This teaching and negative talk will complicate matters for the child, which can affect him or her for the rest of his or her life. Whatever experiences you might have had with a person in the past does not determine that individual will remain the same. People can change for the better, and they often do.

Many Can Make a Baby

There are men and women who can get together in a lustful moment and make a baby, but they might lack the knowledge, wisdom, and character to raise and nurture a child. Instead of focusing on the absent parent or whether you were adopted, you should be grateful that you are here. Invite God into your life and strive to live your best life. It is yours to live; enjoy it while you can.

The thought of what you didn't have from a parent is a negative thought that can engulf your thinking. It will affect your life only in a negative way and manifest things that could not be present. It is like a cut on a person that takes a long time to heal because they keep picking at the wound and saying, "This is sure taking a long time to heal." The individual does not see themselves as the one preventing the healing.

I believe that some of these wounds are unable to heal because many people will not seek counseling, take the advice of a counselor, or use the healing power of forgiveness. The counselor does not have to be a professional; he or she could be a person who has godly wisdom and good common sense.

Because I mention forgiveness, I feel a need to go further in the reasoning and purpose for using this word. I used the word *forgiveness* because I believe in the Genesis account of creation in the Bible, and the

God of the Bible teaches us to seek forgiveness from God and to forgive others.

God created every living thing, including man. God gave Adam instructions to not eat of the tree of knowledge in the Garden of Eden. Eve also was aware of God's instructions; however, Eve looked, desired, and was persuaded to take and eat by the serpent known as Lucifer, Satan, or the devil. She then gave it to Adam, and he ate. Because we have covered the fact that both disobeyed, I will share the remainder of the story directly from the Bible for your reading. Hopefully this will help the reader understand why we need God's forgiveness and why forgiveness of others is so important.

Male and female creation account, their sin and punishment

Let Us Make Man, Male and Female

> Then God said, "Let us make man in our image, in our likeness, and let them rule over the fish of the sea and the birds of the air, over the livestock, over all the earth, and over all the creatures that move along the ground." So God created man in his own image, in the image of God he created him; male and female he created them. (Genesis 1:26–27 NIV)

It is my understanding from these Bible verses that *man* is the term used by God for the human species and that male and female are our genders with which we identify. Males are made different than women, and each one was made by God with specific reasons.

Who Are the Us in Genesis 1:26?

I will use the book of John to explain whom God was talking to when he said, "Let us make man in our image and likeness." This way, the reader will not have to wonder whom God was talking to, just in case you do not know.

> In the beginning was the Word, and the Word was with God, and the Word was God. He was with God in the beginning. Through him all things were made; without him nothing was made that has been made. In him was life, and that life was the light of men. The light shines in the darkness, but the darkness has not understood it. There came a man who was sent from God; his name was John. He came as a witness to testify concerning that light, so that through him all men might believe. He himself was not the light; he came only as a witness to the light. The true light that gives light to every man was coming into the world. He was in the world, and though the world was made through him, the world did not recognize him. He came to that which was his own, but his own did not receive him. Yet to all who received him, to those who believed in his name, he gave the right to become children of God—children born not of natural descent, nor of human decision or a husband's will, but born of God. The Word became flesh and made his dwelling among us. We have seen his glory, the glory of the One and only, who came from the Father, full of grace and truth. John testifies concerning him. He cries out, saying, "This was he of whom I said, 'He who comes after me has surpassed me because he was before me.'" From the fullness of his grace we have all received one blessing after another. For the law was given through Moses; grace and truth came through Jesus Christ. (John 1:1–17 NIV)

God's Punishment to Adam and Eve; Because of Their Disobedience. We all Need God's Forgiveness for Our Sins.

The Lord God took the man and put him in the Garden of Eden to work it and take care of it. And the Lord God commanded the man, "You are free to eat from any tree in the garden. (Genesis 2:15–16 NIV)

Death Is the Penalty for Sin We Need God's Forgiveness for Our Sins

"But you must not eat from the tree of the knowledge of good and evil, for when you eat of it you will surely die." The Lord God said, "It is not good for the man to be alone. I will make a helper suitable for him." Now the Lord God had formed out of the ground all the beasts of the field and all the birds of the air. He brought them to the man to see what he would name them; and whatever the man called each living creature, that was its name. So the man gave names to all the livestock, the birds of the air and all the beasts of the field. (Genesis 2:17–20 NIV)

God Creates Woman

But for Adam no suitable helper was found. So the Lord God caused the man to fall into a deep sleep; and while he was sleeping, he took one of the man's ribs and closed up the place with flesh. Then the Lord God made a woman from the rib he had taken out of the man, and he brought her to the man. The man said, "This is now bone of my bones and flesh of my flesh; she shall be called 'woman, 'for she was taken out of man." For this reason a man will

> leave his father and mother and be united to his wife, and they will become one flesh. (Genesis 2: 21–24 NIV)

Before Sin, They Felt No Shame

> The man and his wife were both naked, and they felt no shame. (Genesis 2: 25 NIV)

Desire and Deception

It is my opinion from this scenario that desire fuels an imaginary sensation associated with the objects of one's desire. Based on the level of strength of the desire and sensation, it creates a mind-set that could cause a person to ignore known consequences and dangers. However, Adam and Eve did not know all that would happen to them before they died, and neither had they had any experience associated with the death of humans or feelings of disobedient to God.

Our Number One Enemy the devil at Work in the Garden

> Now the serpent was more crafty than any of the wild animals the Lord God had made. He said to the woman, "Did God really say, 'You must not eat from any tree in the garden'?" The woman said to the serpent, "We may eat fruit from the trees in the garden, but God did say, 'You must not eat fruit from the tree that is in the middle of the garden, and you must not touch it, or you will die.'" "You will not surely die," the serpent said to the woman. "For God knows that when you eat of it your eyes will be opened, and you will be like God, knowing good and evil." When the woman saw that the fruit of the tree was good for food and pleasing to the eye, and also desirable for gaining wisdom, she took some and ate it. She also

> gave some to her husband, who was with her, and he ate it. (Genesis 3:1–6 NIV)

The Consequences of Adam and Eve's Disobedience

> Then the eyes of both of them were opened, and they realized they were naked; so they sewed fig leaves together and made coverings for themselves. (Genesis 3:7 NIV)

They were not physically blind. It was there, conscious troubling them to the point where they wanted to cover their bodies from each other.

> Then the man and his wife heard the sound of the Lord God as he was walking in the garden in the cool of the day, and they hid from the Lord God among the trees of the garden. But the Lord God called to the man, "Where are you?" He answered, "I heard you in the garden, and I was afraid because I was naked; so I hid." And he said, "Who told you that you were naked? Have you eaten from the tree that I commanded you not to eat from?" The man said, "The woman you put here with me—she gave me some fruit from the tree, and I ate it." Then the Lord God said to the woman, "What is this you have done?" The woman said, "The serpent deceived me, and I ate." (Genesis 3:8–13 NIV)

Punishment for Sin Beginning with the Serpent The Serpent's Punishment for His Part in Initiating This Rebellion

> So the Lord God said to the serpent, "Because you have done this, cursed are you above all the livestock and all the wild animals! You will crawl on your belly and you will eat dust all the days of your life. And I will put enmity

> between you and the woman, and between your offspring and hers; he will crush your head, and you will strike his heel." (Genesis 3:14–15 NIV)

The punishment God issues comes with lasting punishment and no mercy for the serpent. Enmity between the serpent of spring and the woman refers to prophecy. Those who practice the evils perpetrated by Satan are children of darkness. Those who practice the teachings of woman are referring to Jesus, who was born of a woman and brought light to the world through his teachings. This light exposes the evil intents that are hidden in man's heart. Those who follow Jesus's teachings are children of righteousness who walk in the light. Thus, we have the opportunity to observe the holy war that is played out before us in this world. He will crush the serpent's head. He will destroy the serpent, and the serpent will strike his heel. The serpent will strike him with his venom; however, the damage will not be fatal. Jesus and his message continues to save lives and empower all those who believe until he returns.

Her Participation in the Rebellion Causes Childbearing Pain to Increase, and Eve Lost Her Right to Rule beside Adam

> To the woman he said, "I will greatly increase your pains in childbearing; with pain you will give birth to children. Your desire will be for your husband, *and he will rule over you.*" (Genesis 3:16 NIV; emphasis added)

This verse causes me to believe that prior to the rebellion, there wasn't much pain associated with childbirth. God also told Eve that her desire should be for her husband, and he would rule over her. This helped me to understand how the idea of man to rule over woman came into existence. It was a punishment from God on Eve, the female, which has been carried out since the rebellion against God in the beginning of creation.

The Ground Is Cursed because of Adam's Disobedience

> To Adam he said, "Because you listened to your wife and ate from the tree about which I commanded you, 'You must not eat of it.' Cursed is the ground because of you; through painful toil you will eat of it all the days of your life. It will produce thorns and thistles for you, and you will eat the plants of the field. By the sweat of your brow you will eat your food until you return to the ground, since from it you were taken; for dust you are and to dust you will return." Adam named his wife Eve, because she would become the mother of all the living. (Genesis 3:17–18 NIV)

The ground was cursed because of Adam's part in the rebellion. The ground would no longer provide for him with ease what was needed to sustain his life. Pain and toil would be his future for getting from the earth what he needed to survive. In addition to this punishment for Adam, the earth would produce thorns and thistles for him. He would have to work hard for his food, and because he came from the dust, to the dust he would return. Adam's rebellion imputed this punishment to all of man. These punishments were instated by God, and only God's grace and mercy can provide any ease to us.

The Penalty for Sin for All of Us Is Death

Even though Adam and Eve were not put to death by God, an animal was sacrificed to provide a skin covering. What Adam and Eve had made with the leaves for a covering of their bodies was not accepted by God. There is nothing we can do to on our own that will place us in righteous standing with God. God has made a way possible through his son to help us to take care of this matter. An animal had to be sacrificed because of Eve and Adam, and Jesus was a sacrifice for us all.

> The Lord God made garments of skin for Adam and his wife and clothed them. And the Lord God said, "The man has now become like one of us, knowing good and evil. He must not be allowed to reach out his hand and take also from the tree of life and eat, and live forever." So the Lord God banished him from the Garden of Eden to work the ground from which he had been taken. (Genesis 3:21–23 NIV)

Driven from Paradise

> After he drove the man out, he placed on the east side of the Garden of Eden cherubim and a flaming sword flashing back and forth to guard the way to the tree of life. (Genesis 3:24 NIV)

God created every living thing, including man. He gave Adam instructions to not eat of the tree of knowledge in the garden. Eve looked at the tree and desired to eat of it, and with the encouragement of a lie from Satan, she was persuaded to take and eat. The serpent's native language is a lie, and he continues to use his lies on people today.

After she ate, then Adam ate, and the both of them no longer wanted to be seen by God in their nakedness. Neither were they comfortable looking at each other's nakedness. Both of them needed God's forgiveness.

This is how I understand forgiveness to work in a person's life. Forgiveness will allow a person who remembers the moment that a situation occurred where pain was inflicted to him or her. The person will reflect on that moment without connecting the original emotions of pain associated with that moment.

There are those who have not yet become acquainted with the power of forgiveness, and they continue to suffer. The Gospel's message of Jesus has a sure cure for any problem. God, in his divine wisdom, presented to the world his grace and mercy in the word *forgiveness.*

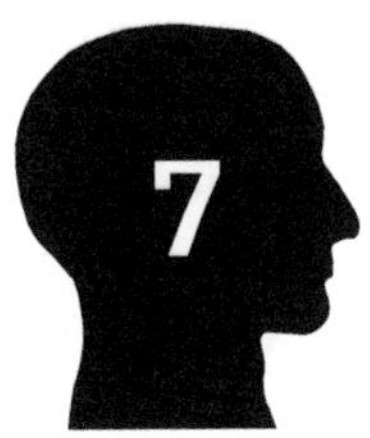

God's plan for mankind and learning to let go of weights

God's Plan for Man Has Always Been Eternal Existence

God's plan for man has always been that of eternal existence with him. If you will read Genesis chapter five, you will find many men who lived over nine hundred years of age. I have added a short list for your viewing.

Genesis 5:5—Adam lived 930 years.
Genesis 5:8—Seth lived 912 years.
Genesis 5:11—Enoch lived 905 years.
Genesis 5:14—Kenan lived 905 years.
Genesis 5:17—Mahalalel lived 895 years.
Genesis 5:20—Jared lived 962 years.
Genesis 5:27—Mathuselah lived 969 years.

From the first man, Adam, to Jesus's sin and death, sin reigned over humanity. But when Jesus died on the cross, he paid the debt that God required for sin. The debt Jesus paid with his life made eternal life possible to all who believe. He was not killed but rather commended his life into his father's hand.

Jesus was buried in a borrowed tomb, where he was for three days. When he arose from the grave, he declared all power to be in his hand. Yshua is his Aramaic name, Iseus is his Greek name, and Jesus is his English name. It was he who made forgiveness possible for all who believe in him. It is important to note that death reigned under the law and that the sacrifice of an animal never cleared the conscious of guilt. Jesus took the power of death away from us and provided his believers with access to eternal life.

Forgiveness Is a Gift to Us
Forgiveness Is God's Gift to Us through His Son, Jesus

> This is my blood of the covenant, which is poured out for many for the forgiveness of sins. (Matthew 26:28–29 NIV)

Jesus's blood was shed for the forgiveness of all men sins. When we believe in Jesus, accept him as our personal savior, and live according to the laws and principles of God's word, he forgives us of our sins. All who face the judgment of God, if not forgiven, will go into the lake of fire along with the devil and all those who rejected the word of God concerning salvation. I have provided for you the following scriptures from Revelation 20.

> And I saw the dead, great and small, standing before the throne, and books were opened. Another book was opened, which is the book of life. The dead were judged according to what they had done as recorded in the books. The sea gave up the dead that were in it, and death and Hades gave up the dead that were in them, and each person was judged according to what he had done. Then death and Hades were thrown into the lake of fire. The lake of fire is the second death. If anyone's name was not found written in the book of life, he was thrown into the lake of fire. (Revelation 20:12–15 NIV)

There will be a day of reckoning and accountability for the things that we have done with the lives that God has given to all of us. Some people may not believe this, and they may choose to live their lives as though there will be no accountability. I was a Boy Scout when I was a child, and one of our mottos was "Be prepared." We need God's forgiveness, and we need to forgive others if we wish to have our names in God's book of life.

The Bible teaches us in the same way that we seek God's forgiveness for trespassing against his laws. We should seek forgiveness from those we have wronged, and we must forgive those who have wronged us.

I want to take a look at what the apostle Paul had to say about carrying unnecessary weights, because that is what I understand these painful memories are like. This is true power in its realest form: I forgive you!

Free Yourself of Unnecessary Burdens

> Therefore, since we are surrounded by such a great cloud of witnesses, let us throw off everything that hinders and the sin that so easily entangles, and let us run with perseverance the race marked out for us. (Hebrews 12:1 NIV)

Paul is addressing people who are of the household of faith and referencing the ones they knew or had heard about what they'd gone through while they were alive. The witnesses are those who endured hardship and made sacrifices because of their belief in the word of God, and they finished the race.

Letting Go of the Weights

I will lead into the following by stating this: what I understand Paul to be referring to as weights are negative thoughts that we hold on to. Because it is held on to by an individual, it can be let go by the same individual. My purpose for publishing this work is to provide insight on steps to take toward letting go of negative thoughts that hurt and hinder.

I have taken many flights on an airplanes and helicopters. One of the things that a commercial airline company requires is that your bags weigh a certain amount, or you will pay a much higher price for each pound over the allotted weight.

All luggage and shipping containers are weighed before they are placed on a plane. They are weighed because the plane can only take off and fly safely with a certain amount of weight. Boats are the same way and are built with a weight capacity.

The air plane pilot needs the plane to fly smoothly and safely in order to reach its destination. The boat captain wants the same to reach his destination. Even the vehicles we drive have towing and weight capacities.

I have watched many movies with ships that encountered a problem that caused them to sink. The first thing they did was try to repair the damage to stop taking on water. If this failed, they would throw things off the boat in an effort to stay afloat and reach land.

In this portion of the text, the apostle provides instructions for us to use in order to get the best out of this life by getting rid of unnecessary loads that we carry in our minds.

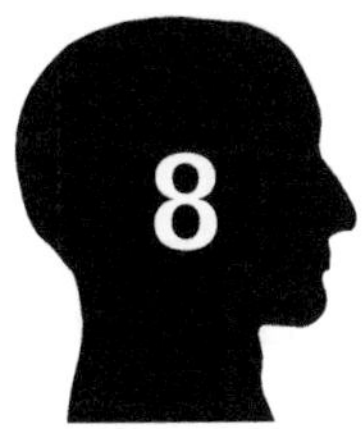

Purposely designed Information and Images of Jesus

Examining a Few Misleading Things That Men Have Presented to the World

In the Hebrew's writings of the apostle Paul, the Spirit of Truth opens the spiritual eyes of the witnesses to the world around them and exposes to them the false values associated with things in this perishing world. The Spirit of Truth will reveal to you the schemes that are in place and that can distract us from pursuing a relationship with our creator. The following are only a few examples that I consider as schemes of men.

For consideration, let's briefly look at the theory of evolution by Charles Robert Darwin. He was born on February 12, 1809, in Shrewsbury, England, and died on April 19, 1882. He was raised in a Christian home. Charles Darwin was an English naturalist, geologist, and biologist best known for his contributions to the science of evolution. His proposition that all species of life have descended over time from common ancestors is now widely accepted and considered a foundational concept in science.

In the 1600s, when the United States came into existence, we believed in the God of the Bible. Prayer was a part of schools' daily curriculum, and we were allowed to take our Bibles to school. The Bible had a great influence in the development of Europe Spain, Rome and the US of

America. "In God We Trust was printed on our money and would share a message wherever these bill went, that we American's Trust in God.

Then came the idea of evolution, which created a sensation that was embraced by the scientific world and later became a part of our education system. This created a shift in many people's belief of the Bible's account of creation and established a belief in evolution for many. This also inspired people like Madalyn Murray O'Hair, an atheist, to start a movement that took a fight all the way to the Supreme Court for the removal of prayer from school. I do not remember hearing of any school shootings before prayer and the Bible were removed. Since the devastating massacre at Columbine High School on April 20, 1999 there have been more than 230 school shootings in the United States

Today there are many known theories and ideas being embraced by many as more and more people disbelieve in the God of the Bible and his teachings.

The media also has a huge amount of influence on us, and it is very important to observe carefully and distinguish what is false and what is true.

The false images of Jesus showing him to be associated with a particular race of people I believe has been purposely done. The oldest painting that I saw of Jesus was found in Syria around 235 BC. From that time on, the dark pictures became lighter pictures. This is the truth: there is only the human race, and in time past history indicates that people were called by the locations where they were citizens. I live in my house on this earth, and wherever I am, I am in my house as a man created in the image of God.

I don't know who or what he looks like, but it really doesn't matter to me. What matters is that anyone who believes in him and accepts him as his or her personal savior becomes a child of God. I personally believe the picture idea was part of a larger conspiracy. The images of Jesus have been supported by many religious denominations around the world. In truth, according to God's law, the images should have ever existed.

The question that I ask myself is how this can be, especially because believers are instructed to not make any images of anything to worship. This was a commandment from God given to Moses for the people of

Israel and to those of the household of faith. I have provided for your reading the following scripture from Exodus, from the New International Version and from the King James Version.

> You shall not make for yourself an idol in the form of anything in heaven above or on the earth beneath or in the waters below. (Exodus 20:4NIV)

> Thou shalt not make unto thee any graven image, or any likeness of anything that is in heaven above, or that is in the earth beneath, or that is in the water under the earth. (Exodus 4:20KJV)

I see these as schemes designed and introduced by individuals and rulers of wickedness in high places, to lead people away from God's truth and use us as puppets.

If we believe the lies and theories that have been presented to us, it would become very easy to not believe in Yahweh and the Bible's account of creation. Many have believed in these new theories and have abandoned the faith. Whatever is stilling your joy and dreams, let it go. Seek the truth, and it will set you free. I have lived with belief in God's word for over fifty-five years.

God has given you what you need to survive. Invite him in so that he can help you get the best out of the time that you have left on this earth. God will help you identify what you need to let go of and give you the strength to turn it loose. Begin by seeking forgiveness from God for your sins and forgiving others. Ask him for his guidance, and he will guide you. Talk to him about your trouble and problems.

> In all your ways acknowledge him, and he will make your paths straight. (Proverbs 3:6 NIV)

When you talk to God, God will respond. When you come to him for help, he will help you.

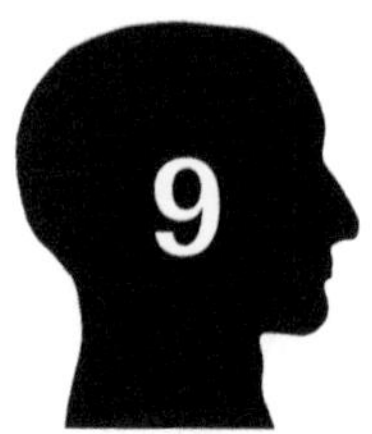

Dangers ways of dealing with unnecessary burdens

Identifying Unnecessary Burdens

I don't understand these weights that Paul was referring to as sins that a person has actually committed. However, I see them as negative thoughts nestle in old memories that a person holds on to from the past. These are thoughts that we hold on to are harmful to our well-being. They are thoughts of the past that we can let go of.

Paul has these instructions for us: to lay aside the weights that hinders us. Paul is careful and precise with the verbiage that he uses while giving these instructions. Mental weights are heavy, and carrying them around can wear you out.

The apostle Paul knew this, and that is why he encouraged us to get rid of them. I recognize that I am more tired after thinking about something negative than when I have worked the same amount of time.

These are some terms to consider as weights, such as *anger*, *hatred*, *jealousy*, *bitterness*, and *vengeance*. I consider these to be huge weights.

When a person is still angry with someone for something that the other did a day ago, a week ago, a month ago, or even years ago, I believe it takes a conscious effort of continual conversations with oneself, revisiting that date and time to keep this feeling alive. It is the same with hatred.

To hold on to hate from a past experience requires a great deal of effort in order to have it in your present. All of the negative emotions that I've mentioned require effort to keep alive. They need to be constantly fed, and guess who is doing the feeding to keep them active?

It is my opinion that hatred toward another person whom I don't know and have never met or had any dealings with is one of the worst types of weights a person can have. I state this because any basis for this is prefabricated on something that I had heard or learned about that person. The truth is I did not know the individual. The same applies to a group of people. I have learned that each individual is unique, even though we all share many of the same desires and our lives are similar in many ways.

My same thoughts would apply when it comes to a group of people. I believe that I am capable of making my own decisions about whom to like without any assistance or outside influences. Simply put, I refused to be a puppet or share a hatred based on lies and others' ideas of that person or group of people.

Allowing any painful emotion of the past to hinder you from becoming the person you were created to be, that is a weight. The past is gone; we only have the present that you and I are in, with hopes of being in tomorrow. There are two days that we cannot do anything in: yesterday and tomorrow. Yesterday is gone, and tomorrow has not arrived. We all can learn from the past and prepare for and build together a better future. In other words, we can learn from the past. I am not making a reference to the history of the pass as it has been presented to us by the US Educational system. Take some time to do some digging and research history for yourself. You just might come across a whole new group of facts to a piece of history that you thought you knew. It is my belief that the history that has been presented to us is the history that the authors wanted us to believe. I have found much new knowledge on history on my own, and this knowledge has provided me with a better understanding of how many things came to be in this world.

Dangerous Ways to Deal with Burdens

We have many old and new thoughts that can reproduce harmful and depressing emotions over and over in our lives. Many of these thoughts have caused a number of people to use and become addicted to prescription or illegal drugs. This approach to get rid of or numb an emotion has proven to be destructive—and even fatal in many cases.

There are many other things that people use to try to silence the memories of a painful past and the present battles of the mind. However, none of these things ever solve the problem within a person. It is a known fact that the use of these things make a bad issue worse. In order to solve the issues, it will have to be dealt with from the inside.

Message from a Doctor's Visit

When people become ill, they can go to a doctor to try to find out what is wrong with their bodies. For some conditions, the doctor can easily identify the problem and prescribe a specific medicine for what he or she believes is the cause of the problem. The medicine may or may not work. There is always the possibility of some type of side effect caused by any medication. If a side effect is recognized due to the medication, the doctor will most likely prescribe a different type of medicine.

Also depending on the reason or reasons of the doctor's visit and the nature of the ailment, an X-ray might be ordered. However, there are other cases where the pinpointing of a problem requires a much more advanced examination.

Here is where a referral might be made for an MRI, which will provide an image of the inside of a human. If the problem is not identified with the MRI, the next referral will be for a CT scan, which will provide a better view of the inside of the body. As you can see, the process of identifying an internal problem can become quite progressive.

Getting to and identifying the root cause of a problem

Mind Dialogue and Owner's Manual

It is my conclusion that it requires prayer, patience, and persistence in order to get to the root cause of a troubled mind. When mental health is the issue, it will require all of the above, along with a good health insurance plan or a huge amount of money, to solve the problem.

When something is wrong in the mind, it affects the spirit and soul, and the only one that can fix what is wrong in those factors is the one who made the mind, spirit, soul, and body. Nothing in this physical world can fix it. We can find answers and solutions to our thinking problems in the words of the owner's manual called the Bible.

Every product that I have ever purchased comes with an owner's manual. The manual provides instructions on how to use the product, warnings against the misuse of the product, and a maintenance schedule regarding how to best service and take care of the product. You will also find information on the best environment for operation and storage.

Getting to the Root Cause of a Problem

God's word can identify exactly where the problem lies in a person and provide the knowledge needed to fix the problem. He is our creator and the provider of our own personal manual. In it, we can find laws for structure and principles to live by that will provide for us a much better way of life.

It is my understanding that a problem is only a problem because I do not have the knowledge I need for a solution. I have learned that seeking council for an understanding on how to fix what I have identified is wrong with me can be very helpful, and wisdom regarding how to use what I have learned and know best can be a sure cure. With God as my guide through the aid of the Holy Spirit, I have found many solutions to my problems with my thinking.

When you have prayed about a problem and searched for a solution over and over in your mind, but you can't find an answer, leave it alone. The answer is not there. Pray about it, and the answer will come. Jesus said in Matthew 7:7–8 NIV, "Ask and it will be given to you; seek and you will find; knock and the door will be opened to you. For everyone who asks receives; he who seeks finds; and to him who knocks, the door will be opened."

I have graduated from believing God's word is true and will accomplish what it says to having the experience of knowing that I can trust his word to do what it proclaims.

> He who is the Glory of Israel does not lie or change his mind; for he is not a man, that he should change his mind. (1 Samuel 15:29 NIV)

The Bible tells us this about the word of God and its ability. However, in order to find out whether or not it is true, one would have to be a believer and a doer. Let us take a look at what the book of James had to say about looking into the Bible and believing and doing what is says.

Be Doers of the Word of God

> But be ye doers of the word, and not hearers only, deceiving your own selves. For if any be a hearer of the word, and not a doer, he is like unto a man beholding his natural face in a glass: For he beholdeth himself, and goeth his way, and straightway forgetteth what manner of man he was. But whoso looketh into the perfect law of liberty, and continueth therein, he being not a forgetful hearer, but a doer of the work, this man shall be blessed in his deed. (James 1:22–25 KJV)

What I have discovered from the word of God is even though it was given to us over thousands of years ago, it identifies things in me that are naturally corrupt and against God's will for my life today.

God word transcends time and space; he is eternal. I learned that I could become a better person by practicing the principles that he has provided and honoring his laws. For me, that was a huge benefit in this life. Let's continue with the book of James and see what he had to say about faith and deeds.

Faith and Deeds Work Together

> What good is it, my brothers, if a man claims to have faith but has no deeds? Can such faith save him? Suppose a brother or sister is without clothes and daily food. If one of you says to him, "Go, I wish you well; keep warm and well fed," but does nothing about his physical needs, what good is it? In the same way, faith by itself, if it is not accompanied by action, is dead. But someone will say, "You have faith; I have deeds." Show me your faith without deeds, and I will show you my faith by what I do. You believe that there is one God. Good! Even the demons believe that—and shudder. You foolish man, do you want

> evidence that faith without deeds is useless? Was not our ancestor Abraham considered righteous for what he did when he offered his son Isaac on the altar? You see that his faith and his actions were working together, and his faith was made complete by what he did. And the scripture was fulfilled that says, "Abraham believed God, and it was credited to him as righteousness," and he was called God's friend. You see that a person is justified by what he does and not by faith alone. (James 2:14–24 NIV)

God's Word Is Alive and Active

> For the word of God is living and active. Sharper than any double-edged sword, it penetrates even to dividing soul and spirit, joints and marrow; it judges the thoughts and attitudes of the heart. Nothing in all creation is hidden from God's sight. Everything is uncovered and laid bare before the eyes of him to whom we must give account. (Hebrews 4:12–13 NIV)

This is what I am hoping this book will do for someone in need who reads the contents. May God truly bless you with the understanding and importance of this message? I believe that this message can transform a person's life for the better.

I have learned from experience that in order to repair or fix what is wrong, one must identify exactly what the root cause of the problem is. Failure to identify and deal with the root cause of the issues will certainly leave an opportunity for future development of pain associated with an old, unresolved problem.

Diagnose and Repair

Think on this for an example. You go outside get in your car and attempt to start it. It is cold outside. A person who has some mechanical experience possibly would assume the battery is dead. This is a common known factor among mechanics and car enthusiasts.

However, making a decision to proceed based on this knowledge alone without running any further tests to identify what the problem is can prove useless. A person could make a trip to the auto parts store to purchase a new battery and install it in the vehicle, drive the car three or four days, and find out it still has the same problem.

This final results will be much time and energy wasted, along with money spent to purchase the wrong item. Sure, maybe you can take the battery back to the store for a refund. But the best scenario in a case like this is to get it right the first time.

Identifying the Root Cause of a Problem

I want to share with you some additional experiences that I have had with getting rid of bushes, weeds, and tree stumps.

In Texas, where I live, there are a lot of unwanted weeds and bushes. We have these mesquite trees that grow everywhere, and they are full of thorns. If you happen to brush against one, you will discover they really can hurt. They can even puncture a tire. I have cut down many just to have them grow right back later. I realized that I needed some help because what I knew and what I was doing weren't working.

I decided to make a trip to a nursery. I realized that I needed some help to solve my problem with these bushes. You see, what I was dealing with was an external problem frustrating me mentally because I had cut them down but they refused to die. I was cutting away what I could see and was not getting rid of the real problem, which was the root. I was unable to see what was underneath the earth. That would need to be dealt with in order to eliminate the item.

The person who I talked with pointed me in the direction of a bunch of chemicals. From that bunch of chemicals, I was instructed to look for and get the one that said "brush killer." I purchased a bottle of brush killer, read the instructions, and followed them. Problem solved. The liquid could travel in the fabric of the bush root system and into the ground where the bush thrived.

I had the same problems with trees that I had cut down, and again I went to the same store and talked to an agent about my tree problem. I was told to go to the area where the chemicals were kept and look for a chemical that read "stump removal." I purchased a bottle, came home, and read the instructions and followed them. My stump problems were solved.

Now, weeds were a whole different breed. I know what to use on weeds. I will spray an area, and the area will change colors and appear dead. Oh, but let a shower come, and out from the dead-looking grass, a sprig will spring forth. When this happens, I will treat the area again until it will not grow back. I have learned from this experience and research on weeds that there are thousands of different types of weeds that the earth can bring forth. Sometimes I had to switch up on chemicals to compensate for the many different types of weeds.

We are similar to the earth in this aspect as it relates to the bushes, stumps, and weeds that were causing me grief. The earth will continue to produce bushes, weeds, and trees. In the same way, life will bring all of us new challenges. I had to deal with them and continue to be vigilant. They won't be the same ones, but I know I have to destroy the roots.

I could not solve my bushes-stumps-and-weeds problem on my own, but I had common sense that said, "Lynn, you need to seek help." It is my understanding that when you occupy a space, it is your responsibility to maintain that space, whether it's internal or external. Failure to do so will result in whatever it is that you neglect eventually overtaking you.

As I visited my hometown over the years, I noticed houses, buildings, and my old school in deteriorating condition. Trees, weeds, and bushes were now in areas where children used to play. Places where we used to shop were in the same condition. Walls were leaning, windows were broken, roofs were caved in, and nature was taking over the land. One lot where my sister had a house at one time was completely covered with trees, bushes, and weeds. It was as though a house had never been there.

A Little Yeast

That brings me to this point: a little yeast in flour and water will leaven the whole lump. Red Kool-Aid in a glass of water will change the color of the water. Therefore it is necessary to immediately identify what is the cause of any mental or emotional problem so that the problem is not something that you will have present for the rest of your life.

Problems within any individual on a personal level will affect his or her personality, character, and relationships with other people.

I have found myself asking these questions: What is it about some humans who are warned of a threat that could take their lives but do not take heed of the warning? Why can't an individual who is on a path of destruction not understand his or her condition and change?

I know that there are some people who are mentally unable to understand the dangers of what they are doing. I have met others who seem to have all their mental faculties in order and who when warned still continue on a path of destruction.

Mind conflict is our worst enemy, and that is something all of us can work on in order to have the best lives possible and better relationships with others.

Focus on factual thoughts, prepare for Satan's attacks and be alert

Focus on the Facts

It is my belief that people need to begin by focusing on facts that are associated with any thoughts that they may have before they speak or act. Every thought that we have that is not supported by facts is simply a random thought and nothing more.

We have thousands of thoughts that will go through our minds throughout a day. Many of these thoughts are negative, and in the midst of these thoughts, we often think about individuals. Some thoughts are not good thoughts and usually are not based on facts. If people are not careful, they can find themselves disliking an individual for no reasons other than their own thoughts.

I woke up on the morning of December 15, 2010, at six o'clock, and I believe the Lord gave me some insight concerning our physical and spiritual makeup and things that each one of us can do to deal with the conflicts that arise between the two.

We have a mind, body, and spirit, and in this life, we will have many decisions to make and things to do.

One important factor that many of us will omit or may not even consider is that we have an enemy that is filled with fury toward us. Our number one enemy is the devil. He was with God before you and I came into existence, and he knows firsthand what it was like to be with him. He messed up, and he is a prodigal son who can never return home.

He caused Adam and Eve to sin in the beginning of time, and his mission and tactics remains the same today and will continue until God brings closure. He and all who believe in him are on a short trip to the lake of fire, where his existence will be extinguished.

Not so with you and I those of the household of faith. Jesus made a way possible for us to be reconnected to God and regain access to eternal life. The devil deceived Eve and Adam, and he might have thought he had done something to thwart God's plan for mankind. He even went as far as to try to kill Jesus, but Jesus laid down his life, took the power of death away, and ushered in grace and mercy. This grace is not extended to Satan.

He failed in every attempt to destroy Jesus and his message, but he continues to work on destroying the human race, God's offspring.

He continues to use his same methods of lying and deception. When a person embraces the idea that this life experience is all that it is, the devil has that person in his grasp. When a person does not believe in the Bible, the devil has that person in his grasp. I have talked with many individuals who have other faiths and religious beliefs. During these conversations, almost all the time the Bible usually gets attacked.

Prepare for Satan's Attacks

Therefore put on the whole armor of God and stand firm in your mind. It may look like you won't make it, but that is the kind of thought that the devil hopes you believe. The apostle Paul gives us instructions on how to prepare and be ready for an attack from the enemy in the book of Ephesians.

> Finally, be strong in the Lord and in his mighty power. Put on the full armor of God so that you can take your stand against the devil's schemes. For our struggle is not against flesh and blood, but against the rulers, against

> the authorities, against the powers of this dark world and against the spiritual forces of evil in the heavenly realms. Therefore put on the full armor of God, so that when the day of evil comes, you may be able to stand your ground, and after you have done everything, to stand. Stand firm then, with the belt of truth buckled around your waist, with the breastplate of righteousness in place, and with your feet fitted with the readiness that comes from the gospel of peace. In addition to all this, take up the shield of faith, with which you can extinguish all the flaming arrows of the evil one. Take the helmet of salvation and the sword of the Spirit, which is the word of God. And pray in the Spirit on all occasions with all kinds of prayers and requests. With this in mind, be alert and always keep on praying for all the saints. (Ephesians 6:10–18 NIV)

Be Self-Controlled and Alert

I have a good understating of the importance of being alert. I worked at Parchman, a correctional facility in Mississippi, as a security guard in a tower on the outside the maximum security unit and later inside. I also served in the army in the air cavalry unit. These are places where my life depended on my being alert at all times. While in the army, I was trained to be placed near, or get as close as possible to, the enemy without compromising my presence. This is how, I could spy on their movement and know what they were up to so that we could alert other parts of our unit.

The Bible teaches us in 1 Peter 5:8–9 NIV, "Be self-controlled and alert. Your enemy the devil prowls around like a roaring lion looking for someone to devour. Resist him, standing firm in the faith, because you know that your brothers throughout the world are undergoing the same kind of sufferings."

There is great value in being self-controlled and alert. Being self-controlled will prevent a person from being carried off emotionally by any random thought. Being alert is like a watchman on a post in a war zone: their eyes and their ears are sharp to any movement or sound. It is vital to their continued existence.

We should think the same way as the watchman over our souls.

I have listened and talked to so many people with so many different problems from their pasts. They could not seem to get over things, and that affected their lives today in a negative way. What I have learned from these conversations is that many people use a Band-Aid approach, and that is to use something for the moment to massage the pain. The wound is still there and will not heal because they fail to use the right solution.

There are people who have counseled others with healing words but will not use what they say on themselves.

I understand this to be true because I could have the same conversation with some of the same people over and over again if I would participate. This scenario happens because the individual did not apply what was shared to them on the root cause of his or her issue.

If I have a toothache, I will go to a dentist, and if it can be fixed, I will have the dentist fix the tooth. If the tooth is beyond repair, he will have to extract the tooth. Either way, the problem is solved.

In an effort to help oneself, there are some things that I believe one needs to plunge into and take a look at, and that is my attempt with the contents of this book, to provide helpful information. I hope that this information will shed light where it is needed in the lives of those who will take the time to read its contents.

In order to fix our problems, we need to understand how we were designed and by whom.

The body was made as a dwelling for this world, the soul is whoever you are, and the spirit is life from God. The voice that you hear on the inside is you. For the voice that interrupts the conversation that we have going on with ourselves and gives us good advice, good instructions, and warnings, I understand that voice to be the voice of reasoning provided by the Holy Spirit.

He won't lead you to a place where things will not work out for your good. The other instructions that are against the word of God might be from the carnal man or a negative word delivered to us by the devil.

The devil tempted Jesus after he had fasted forty days and forty nights, using suggestive statements. He knew that Jesus was hungry, and he told him to turn some stones to bread. First of all, Jesus wasn't supposed to take any orders from him, and second, bread was not made from stone. Jesus had been in the wilderness alone for forty days without food and water. Yet, when the tempter came to him offering to him what the body desperately needed and what the carnal man desperately desires, Jesus resisted and use the word of God.

Therefore any suggestions or instructions from the devil to us should always be ignored because he is the father of lies. Resist him and he will flee.

Internal and external body parts and purposes

God Created Man

> The Lord God formed the man from the dust of the ground and breathed into his nostrils the breath of life, and the man became a living being. (Genesis 2:7 NIV)

The book of Genesis, provides us an account of creation. When God created plants, he spoke to the earth. When he created animals, he spoke to the earth. When he created the stars, the sun, and the moon, he spoke to the elements in the air. When he created fish, he spoke to the waters.

When it came to man, he spoke to himself, and to Jesus and said, "Let us make them in our likeness and image." He breathed into man life. Man is the species, and male and female is the gender. He created us in his class. Yes, you and I were created in God's class. We have the ability to think, imagine, create visions, and bring them into existence. This is some good stuff.

Let's take a broader look. Every new store, every new car, every new house, every new computer, every new phone, every new design of clothes—all were in someone's mind before they came into existence. What are your weights holding you back from doing things?

When God finished breathing life into us, we were complete. Each new sunrise that you experience presents you with a new opportunity.

The living soul became an individual, with each one of us having an identity of our own and the ability to choose. Every choice ends with a decision and every decisions brings about consequences. Just as we choose to do things that we have tried and learn to satisfy the emotions of the physical, God has introduced to us an excellent way of choosing to live life, as well as life everlasting. Learn to listen to him when he speaks.

The body is made up of many parts; it is visible and needs food, water, and air to survive. The devil wants us to use our bodies in service to him in this corrupted world, and he will gain control of a person if he or she allows him to do so.

In the Bible, Paul gives us these instructions on what to do with our bodies. If we follow his instructions, it will provide us with the necessary environment for us to be successful.

What you have done and what has happened to you in the past does not dictate your future. There is greatness in you that God placed there, and it is called potential.

I must tell you this potential needs a purpose and purpose places demand on potential.

> Therefore, I urge you, brothers, in view of God's mercy, to offer your bodies as living sacrifices, holy and pleasing to God—this is your spiritual act of worship. Do not conform any longer to the pattern of this world, but be transformed by the renewing of your mind. Then you will be able to test and approve what God's will is—his good, pleasing and perfect will. (Romans 12: 1–2 NIV)

Change is a mind-altering experience. Whatever condition that a person is in mentally and emotionally, it took them some time to get to that point. Therefore establish a mindset steadfastness. This is a step-by-step process, that may prove to be changeling and you can make it. Remind yourself that quitting is not an option.

The Body Consists of Internal and External Components

Internal Parts

The heart is a muscle that pumps blood through the body.
The liver is the organ that secretes enzymes that break down food so that the body can use them.
The kidneys filter and clean whatever you ingest for the cells in the body and gets rid of impurities in the form of urine.
The lungs are responsible for inhaling oxygen for the body and exhaling carbon dioxide.
The bladder is a storage area for the urine.
The spleen is a graveyard for dead red blood cells.
The stomach is for digesting food.
The gallbladder stores the bile that the liver produces, and it also helps break down fat.
The pancreas assists with the digesting of food and also controls blood sugar levels.
The small intestines are for digestion and absorption of food for the body.
The large intestine is used for storage of waste and an exit.

External Parts

We have a head, two eyes, two ears, one nose, one neck, one chest, one stomach, two shoulders, two arms, two hands, ten fingers, two legs, two knees, two ankles, and two feet with ten toes. All the organs and parts work together in an automatic process for the well-being of the body. Its blueprint was designed by God to be used in this world. God's word gives us instructions on how to take care of this body and rule in it with the authority that he has given to each one of us. When we disobey what he has instructed us, we can cause harm to it, or we can choose to do things that will destroy it, shorten our time in this world, and prevent us from entering the new world to come, all because of disobedience.

When we fail to adhere to the voice of true counseling, we can create things that will bring pain to us (the soul) as well as harm to the body. When the circumstances that we create from the decisions that we make cause a painful lasting memory, we have to live with the memory from those situations and deal with the circumstances.

The failure to listen to the voice of reasoning provided by the Holy Spirit or one of God's messengers could possibly be the beginning of a new painful experience and ongoing conversation. It's one that plays out like this: "I wish I had listened. I hate that I did this or that." Sentences like these are constant reminders that lead to painful memories and emotions, anger, disappointment, frustration, depression, and low self-esteem. Quite often they are rooted somewhere in a person's past.

Many of these emotional feelings and nagging, annoying memories we just can't seem to get rid of. Often one will go to the doctor to try and find some kind of medication to numb the feelings caused by the voice, but the voice of the memory remains.

Some people may choose to use alcohol, drugs, sex, pornography, or other methods to numb these negative thoughts, only to realize that they have to continue the behavior while their thoughts and emotions remain the same. Then one day, when they accept that they are powerless and tired of this condition, they decide to reach out for help. The conversation with solicitation for help is introduced again with that same voice that told them to not do what they did or were contemplating doing.

Many times, people are not able to recognize this other person on the inside talking to them with words that have warnings and positive directions. It's the Holy Spirit, and He is the one that will encourage you to go to church, pray, read your Bible and join a church as well. When you are emotional struggling with past memories and life I encourage you to ask God for forgiveness and help. Once people humble and surrender control of their lives and seek God's help, they will find help. Maybe a talk with God in a time of emotional despair will save a life. Keep in mind that you can force Jesus away from the position of head of your life by doing what you want to do.

External Parts of the Body

In the natural the eyes are used to send pictures to the brain; however, the soul identifies what it is and then names it. I believe that it is the same as in the beginning, when God gave Adam the responsibility of naming all of the animals.

The ears are used for capturing sound for us; however, we give identity to the sound.
The nose is used for smelling, bringing in air, and exhaling.
The mouth is used for bringing in air and exhaling, holding food, and talking.
The tongue is used for taste, moving things around in our mouths, and speech.
The fingers are used to grasp and pick up things, push buttons, turn knobs, and feel.
The toes help balance us while we are walking.
The body houses all of our internal organs.
The soul of a person is the personality and character of an individual. The thing that I have learned is the character that I portray and my personality is all mine.

God purposely Made Men and women physically different.

All of these external body parts have specific functions and sensations. However, the mind is the control center for the entire being. Therefore the body should never be the driver of your life choices but rather the passenger.

Walk in Righteousness

Do not worry about what others might think when you choose to walk in the pathway of righteousness. "Do not be afraid of those who kill the body but cannot kill the soul. Rather, be afraid of the One who can destroy both soul and body in hell" (Matthew 10:28 NIV).

God is the only one that can destroy the soul. Man can harm the body to the point that he will not be able to use his arm, feet, legs, hands, eyes, or ears. This would mean that no matter what a soul wanted to do if the parts are there, if the senses cannot make the connection for them to act; they won't work.

However, even in this condition, there can be peace on the inside because of the comfort that comes from the presence of God. This is the place where each one of us should be striving to be, and that is in the comfort of God's presence, trusting in him to work things out for us by knowing the following words.

Walk in righteousness and God will provide for and protect you

If God Is for Us

> What, then, shall we say in response to this? If God is for us, who can be against us? (Romans 8:31 NIV) God has our back our sides and our front, we are well protected in his care. As in the case of Job when the Devil wanted to have his way with him he need permission.
>
> Have you not put a hedge around him and his household and everything he has? You have blessed the work of his hands, so that his flocks and herds are spread throughout the land. (Job 1:10 NIV)

Greater is he who is in us.

> Ye are of God, little children, and have overcome them: because greater is he that is in you, than he that is in the world. (1 John 4:4 NIV)

There is no power in the world greater than God, our creator.

No Weapon Forged against Us Will Prevail

> No weapon forged against you will prevail and you will refute every tongue that accuses you. This is the heritage of the servants of the Lord, and this is their vindication from me," declares the Lord. (Isaiah 54:17 NIV)

This is a promise that God made to those that are obedient to the Lord.

> A generous man will prosper; he who refreshes others will himself be refreshed. (Proverbs 11:25 NIV)

> He who conceals his sins does not prosper, but whoever confesses and renounces them finds mercy. (Proverbs 28:13 NIV)

> For I know the plans I have for you," declares the Lord, "plans to prosper you and not to harm you, plans to give you hope and a future. (Jeremiah 29:11 NIV)

> Then the Spirit of God came upon Zechariah son of Jehoiada the priest. He stood before the people and said, "This is what God says: 'Why do you disobey the Lord's commands? You will not prosper. Because you have forsaken the Lord, he has forsaken you.'" (2 Chronicles 24:20 NIV)

> What good will it be for a man if he gains the whole world, yet forfeits his soul? (Matthew 16:26 NIV)

If your only ambition is to obtain material things in this life to make you happy, how do you feel when you think about how you are going to die and leave it all behind?

What if one day, when you cease to exist here, you find yourself in the presence of God to answer for what you did with your life? What would be your answer knowing that you rejected the message of salvation?

One would need to believe in God's son, Jesus, in this world and learn to love as he did. Learn his teachings and obey them. I like what James had to say in James 1:22–25 NIV.

> Do not merely listen to the word, and so deceive yourselves. Do what it says. Anyone who listens to the word but does not do what it says is like a man who looks at his face in a mirror and, after looking at himself, goes away and immediately forgets what he looks like. But the man who looks intently into the perfect law that gives freedom, and continues to do this, not forgetting what he has heard, but doing it—he will be blessed in what he does.

When people examine their own selves by their standards or someone else's standards that will lead to a false perception of their selves. Here is what I find to be a reason for this false perception. Every one of us is right in our own thinking, and we were not made to be like someone else—we were made to be ourselves. Therefore in order to be the best me that I can be, I need to follow my manufacturer's instructions and example for my life.

The Bible message and Jesus teachings

The Bible Message

The Bible is a book that has been provided to us though many great sacrifices. I am not sure of the thoughts by humans, if any has been given to this matter, regarding the amazement of this wonderful book and all that it has to offer us. What has the Bible gone through and survived and the lives that were punished or taken because they believe in it and shared the salvation message?

I think of the prophets who were killed in the Bible's history and the many announcements about the coming Messiah. Which I would have thought would have provided a welcome arrival to his people and religious leaders of his people. Contrary to this opinion, a king wanted Jesus dead after his birth.

The chief priest Caiaphas, along with the Pharisees, Sadducees, and the Herodians wanted Jesus killed. They had Pilate, a Roman governor, order his crucifixion. Many of his twelve disciples were murdered, and the remaining followers were persecuted. One might say, "Who would want to be associated with such a group of believers?"

Yet the Bible prevailed for thousands of years through much adversity, and its power is as potent today as it was when it was first transcribed. It is still changing lives and saving souls.

Jesus's Teachings Came with Authority and Power

The teachings of Jesus came with authority and power, and that is what we need words that are alive.

> When the crowds heard this, they were astonished at his teaching. Hearing that Jesus had silenced the Sadducees, the Pharisees got together. One of them, an expert in the law, tested him with this question: "Teacher, which is the greatest commandment in the Law?" (Matthew 22:33–36 NIV)
>
> Jesus replied: "Love the Lord your God with all your heart and with all your soul and with all your mind." This is the first and the greatest commandment. And the second is like it: Love your neighbor as yourself. All the Law and the prophets hang on these two commandments. (Matthew 22:37- 40)

Let's look at what the Bible has to say about love. We use the phrase "I love you" so freely, but do we really understand what it means and the power that it possesses?

Love

> If I speak in the tongues of men and of angels, but have not love, I am only a resounding gong or a clanging cymbal. If I have the gift of prophecy and can fathom all mysteries and all knowledge, and if I have a faith that can move mountains, but have not love, I am nothing. If

I give all I possess to the poor and surrender my body to the flames, but have not love, I gain nothing.

Love is patient, love is kind. It does not envy, it does not boast, it is not proud. It is not rude, it is not self-seeking, it is not easily angered, it keeps no record of wrongs. Love does not delight in evil but rejoices with the truth. It always protects, always trusts, always hopes, and always perseveres.

Love never fails. But where there are prophecies, they will cease; where there are tongues, they will be stilled; where there is knowledge, it will pass away. For we know in part and we prophesy in part. (1 Corinthians 13:1–9 NIV)

When you fall in love with Jesus, you will want to honor him, and you will be delighted to turn the controls of your life over to him. Sit back, relax, and enjoy the journey through life.

Think about where you are in life and what you are doing. Take another look at the meaning of love; you might need to put into practice some of the things that you have just read. You might even lose a ton of weight. Halleluiah!

The Spirit Gives Life from God

With our eyes, we see things; with our nose, we smell things; with our ears, we hear things; with our mouths, we taste things; with our mouths, we also talk. I believe the brain processes this information, but the soul identifies what we have learned. I name it based on what I (the soul) understand it to be. The counselor (the Holy Spirit) will be my guide with the information that I will obtain in life and will help me to understand and give me wisdom.

15 Processing knowledge and using discernment

Processing Knowledge and Thoughts

Not all knowledge is beneficial to us, and therefore we need to learn the tremendous value of his help. I understand the body being like a touch pad, sending signals of things that it comes into contact with to the brain, whether it's wet, dry, cold, hot, or pain. I believe that the brain separates what it collects and distributes to different compartments to be identified and kept ether in short-term or long-term memory. The soul is where thoughts ideas and feelings are made sense of. This understanding takes shape in our thoughts.

My wife and I have looked at the same piece of clothing when we were getting dress for church, and I identified a piece of clothing as one color and my wife identified the same piece of clothing being a different color from what I saw. At some point in our minds, the process results are viewed as differently.

The soul (me) sits in the seat of authority in my thoughts as a spiritual part of my being, and my brain constantly receives and processes the information that is being transmitted. Then I decide what should be done with it. It is at this point the Holy Spirit will speak to me and help me to understand what choice is my best path. Sometimes we are still not sure what to do, and God will place a person on our minds, or he may direct us to someone who can give us clarity concerning a matter. It is up to us to use what we will learn or not.

My ears are on the outside of my head, listening. Then how am I hearing on the inside of me a voice when I am not in the company of anyone? When I am alone, even when I am watching TV, when I'm listing to the radio, or when I'm talking to someone, I can still hear this voice on the inside. As a matter of fact, he is always talking. Sometimes I am able to sit and listen to him, and he makes good sense; sometime he just babbles. These thoughts are different from those provide by the Holy Spirit.

Discerning My Thoughts

Over time, I have learned how to distinguish between the voices by examining the value of the contents of the thoughts. Most important of all, this voice tells me what to do when certain body parts send a signal to the brain. For example, when my bladder is full, there is a message sent to the brain that I (the soul) examine and let the body know the necessary action it needs to take. I am the one who will have to tell it what to do or where it needs to go, and it obeys. As I use the term voice and voices it is actually more like me generating and reading thoughts that enter my mind.

I like what Apostle Paul had to say about taking control of his body.

> Do you not know that in a race all the runners run, but only one gets the prize? Run in such a way as to get the prize. Everyone who competes in the games goes into strict training. They do it to get a crown that will not last; but we do it to get a crown that will last forever. Therefore I do not run like a man running aimlessly; I do not fight like a man beating the air. No, I beat my body and make it my slave so that after I have preached to others, I myself will not be disqualified for the prize. (1 Corinthians 9:24–27 NIV)

I understand the soul of a man being the most valuable part of him. The soul will not die, and we learn from the word of God that the soul is priceless. It is the soul that will be judged, it is the soul that will receive a new name, and it is the soul that loves the Lord. It is also my understanding that our souls will be housed in bodies like those of the angels, and that the faithful in this life will never die.

The Avatar scene and the war within

The Scene from *Avatar*

The best way that I can think of explaining this is from a scene in the movie *Avatar*. They had this man who was a crippled marine, and they placed him in a piece of equipment. He went to sleep, and though he was not able to fully use his body because he was paralyzed from waist down, his being was transported into the other body of an avatar made for that planet, and he was fully functional.

Also in *Avatar*, there is this military commander who has a large robot that he is able to get into and control its every move. I understand each one of us to be like this commander: we sit at the controls of our bodies. In addition, we are the true commanders of our bodies. The following scriptures provide us with further instructions of guidance for our bodies.

> Dear friends, I urge you, as aliens and strangers in the world, to abstain from sinful desires, which war against your soul. (1 Peter 2:11 NIV)

These sinful desires are given birth by thoughts or desires that once they are acted on have given birth to the physical hidden sin of man but not hidden from God because he knows our every thought.

The War Within, Written by Paul

We know that the law is spiritual; but I am unspiritual, sold as a slave to sin. I do not understand what I do. For what I want to do I do not do, but what I hate I do. And if I do what I do not want to do, I agree that the law is good. As it is, it is no longer I myself who do it, but it is sin living in me. I know that nothing good lives in me, that is, in my sinful nature. For I have the desire to do what is good, but I cannot carry it out. For what I do is not the good I want to do; no, the evil I do not want to do—this I keep on doing. Now if I do what I do not want to do, it is no longer I who do it, but it is sin living in me that does it.

So I find this law at work: When I want to do good, evil is right there with me. For in my inner being I delight in God's law; but I see another law at work in the members of my body, waging war against the law of my mind and making me a prisoner of the law of sin at work within my members. What a wretched man I am! Who will rescue me from this body of death? Thanks be to God—through Jesus Christ our Lord!

So then, I myself in my mind am a slave to God's law, but in the sinful nature a slave to the law of sin. (Romans 7:14–25 NIV)

The Battle Must Be Fought and Won in Our Minds

Here I am! I stand at the door and knock. If anyone hears my voice and opens the door, I will come in and eat with him, and he with me. (Revelation 3:20 NIV)

“This is my thought after reading the above scripture.” What is this phrase saying to us? Is it saying that we should be listening for an audible sound with our ears, or is it talking about the soul, which has no physical ears but is constantly busy except when he is asleep? The soul does have the ability to hear from the spiritual world because of its design.

Opening the door to allow Jesus requires an inside decisions

Behold, I Stand at the Door and Knock

"Behold, I stand at the door and knock:" if any man hear my voice, and open the door, I will come in to him, and sup with him and he with me. (Revelation 3:20 NIV). "Behold, I stand at the door and knock:" There are many sayings of this kind among the ancient rabbis. Thus in Shir Hashirim Rabba, fol. 25, 1, God said to the Israelites, "My children, open to me one door of repentance, even so wide as the eye of a needle, and I will open to you doors through which calves and horned cattle may pass."

In Sohar Levit, fol. 8, col. 32, it is said,

> If a man conceal his sin, and do not open it before the holy King, although he ask mercy, yet the door of repentance shall not be opened to him. But if he open it before the holy blessed God, God spares him, and mercy prevails over wrath; and when he laments, although all the doors were shut, yet they shall be opened to him, and his prayer shall be heard.

> Christ stands-waits long, at the door of the sinner's heart; he knocks-uses judgments, mercies, reproofs, exhortations, etc., to induce sinners to repent and turn to him; he lifts up his voice-calls loudly by his word, ministers, and Spirit.
>
> [If any man hear] If the sinner will seriously consider his state, and attend to the voice of his Lord.
>
> [And open the door] This must be his own act, receiving power for this purpose from his offended Lord, who will not break open the door; he will make no forcible entry. He will only come in by invitation.
>
> [I will come in to him] I will manifest myself to him, heal all his backslidings, pardon all his iniquities, and love him freely.
>
> [Will sup with him] Hold communion with him, feed him with the bread of life.
>
> [And He with me.] I will bring him at last to dwell with me in everlasting glory.

From Adam Clarke's Commentary Electronic Data Base

He will give us words to lead us, protect us, help us, heal us, and comfort us. He will give us ideas with which to prosper.

Paul said to Timothy, "Consider what I say; and the Lord give thee understanding in all things" (2 Timothy 2:7 NIV). In other words, what you read and what you hear from God's word, think about it and meditate on for a deeper meaning and understanding. Ask yourself, "Can this help me? Could this make me a better person if I were to honor what the word said? Could my actions on what his word says to me prevent me from walking into or creating chaos for my life?"

Reflecting back on a portion from Adams Clark commentary:

> [And he with me.] I will bring him at last to dwell with me in everlasting glory.

He will bring you into everlasting glory. He is not talking about our physical bodies. God will bring our souls, into everlasting glory the entity of our being. As Christians, we are to bring our bodies into subjection of the words of Jesus Christ.

In the Beginning Was the Word

> In the beginning was the Word, and the Word was with God, and the Word was God. He was with God in the beginning. Through him all things were made; without him nothing was made that has been made. In him was life, and that life was the light of men. The light shines in the darkness, but the darkness has not understood it. (John 1:1–5 NIV)

> He was in the world, and though the world was made through him, the world did not recognize him. He came to that which was his own, but his own did not receive him. Yet to all who received him, to those who believed in his name, he gave the right to become children of God—children born not of natural descent, nor of human decision or a husband's will, but born of God. The Word became flesh and made his dwelling among us. We have seen his glory, the glory of the One and only, who came from the Father, full of grace and truth. (John 1:10–14 NIV)

Today, we hear his word physically through our ears and we read his word physically with our eyes. From this process it up to the one in charge of the body to decide what will be done. It will be your decision whether to honor what you have heard or read from the word of God.

God loves each one of us, and that is why he allowed his son to die on the cross. Jesus loves us, and that is why he was willing to die to pay a debt for sin that He did not owe. The process in getting to know him will not be found by searching for a religion but a kingdom.

So do not worry, saying, "What shall we eat?" or "What shall we drink?" or "What shall we wear?" For the pagans run after all these things, and your heavenly Father knows that you need them. But seek first his kingdom and his righteousness, and all these things will be given to you as well. (Matthew 6:31–33 NIV)

Steps to help the new believer to enter God's Kingdom

How to Enter into the Kingdom of God and What We Must Do

1. You must be born again.

> In reply Jesus declared, "I tell you the truth, no one can see the kingdom of God unless he is born again." (John 3:3 NIV)

The term "born again" has to do with a change that is in our thinking. For many, this might mean a change in doing everything different, and for others it might mean a change in only a few things.

This change will be manifested to all who know you and the way you used to be because of the new way you have learned to deal with matters and live. For example, if everyone around a person had labeled him a thief and a liar because that is the type of behavior he or she practiced, and they stopped, people would notice a difference in behavior. To further emphasize this matter, I will discuss it under number two.

2. You must offer your body as a living sacrifice.

> Therefore, I urge you, brothers, in view of God's mercy, to offer your bodies as living sacrifices, holy and pleasing to God—this is your spiritual act of worship. Do not conform any longer to the pattern of this world, but be transformed by the renewing of your mind. Then you will be able to test and approve what God's will is—his good, pleasing and perfect will. (Romans 12:1–2 NIV)

It is by the surrendering control of our will over our bodies unto God, through the Holy Spirit. We do this because of belief and faith in the price that Jesus paid by dying on the cross for our sins. We participate in the practicing of the Bible's principles so that we will be able to test and understand what his will is for our lives.

3. You must repent (ask God for his forgiveness).

This means that when one realizes the truth in God's word, one would feel a genuine sorrow for their actions and ask him for his forgiveness, and from that moment on live obeying his word.

> In those days John the Baptist came, preaching in the Desert of Judea 2 and saying, "Repent, for the kingdom of heaven is near." (Matthew 3:1 NIV)

4. You must be baptized in the name of Jesus Christ for the forgiveness of your sins.

> Peter replied, "Repent and be baptized, every one of you, in the name of Jesus Christ for the forgiveness of your sins. And you will receive the gift of the Holy Spirit. The promise is for you and your children and for all who are far off—for all whom the Lord our God will call." (Acts 2:38–39 NIV)

Jesus himself was baptized by John.

> As soon as Jesus was baptized, he went up out of the water. At that moment heaven was opened, and he saw the Spirit of God descending like a dove and lighting on him. And a voice from heaven said, "This is my Son, whom I love; with him I am well pleased." (Matthew 3:16–17 NIV)

> I would not have known him, except that the one who sent me to baptize with water told me, 'The man on whom you see the Spirit come down and remain is he who will baptize with the Holy Spirit.' I have seen and I testify that this is the Son of God." (John 1:33–34 NIV)

The Holy Spirit is God and Jesus's gift to all who believe and obey his teachings. The Holy Spirit is how God speaks to our souls (to us) with words of comfort, with words of instructions, and with words of discipline.

These words are meant to help us and not to harm us. These words, when obeyed, will help us in many ways. Try obeying them, and you will see the results they will bring. The longer you listen to him and the more you talk to him, the better you will understand the God we serve, who is our creator.

5. Sanctify yourself.

May God himself, the God of peace, sanctify you through and through. May your whole spirit, soul and body be kept blameless at the coming of our Lord Jesus Christ? The one who calls you is faithful and he will do it. (1 Thessalonians 5:23–24 NIV) Chose to live a life that is a replica of the character of Jesus. I see sanctification as a process that occurs over time, whereby a person spontaneously or gradually remove from their life the things that they were doing against the will of God.

6. Crucify the old self.

> For we know that our old self was crucified with him so that the body of sin might be done away with, that we should no longer be slaves to sin. (Romans 6:6 NIV)

When we accept Jesus in to our lives, we stop doing the things that we have learned that were against the teachings found in the Bible. Letting go of or stop practicing old habits can be painful, thus established a since of crucifying of the flesh.

7. Transform your mind into a new way of thinking. Read God's word, learn it, and obey the teachings.

> Surely you heard of him and were taught in him in accordance with the truth that is in Jesus. You were taught, with regard to your former way of life, to put off your old self, which is being corrupted by its deceitful desires; to be made new in the attitude of your minds; and to put on the new self, created to be like God in true righteousness and holiness. (Ephesians 4:21–24 NIV)

8. Learn and practice the kingdom life style.

> Therefore each of you must put off falsehood and speak truthfully to his neighbor, for we are all members of one body. "In your anger do not sin": Do not let the sun go down while you are still angry, and do not give the devil a foothold. He who has been stealing must steal no longer, but must work, doing something useful with his own

hands, that he may have something to share with those in need. Do not let any unwholesome talk come out of your mouths, but only what is helpful for building others up according to their needs, that it may benefit those who listen. And do not grieve the Holy Spirit of God, with whom you were sealed for the day of redemption. Get rid of all bitterness, rage and anger, brawling and slander, along with every form of malice. Be kind and compassionate to one another, forgiving each other, just as in Christ God forgave you. (Ephesians 4:25–32 NIV)

9. Imitate God as children (be humble).

Be imitators of God, therefore, as dearly loved children and live a life of love, just as Christ loved us and gave himself up for us as a fragrant offering and sacrifice to God.

But among you there must not be even a hint of sexual immorality, or of any kind of impurity, or of greed, because these are improper for God's holy people. Nor should there be obscenity, foolish talk or coarse joking, which are out of place, but rather thanksgiving. For of this you can be sure: No immoral, impure or greedy person—such a man is an idolater—has any inheritance in the kingdom of Christ and of God. Let no one deceive you with empty words, for because of such things God's wrath comes on those who are disobedient. Therefore do not be partners with them.

For you were once darkness, but now you are light in the Lord. Live as children of light (for the fruit of the light consists in all goodness, righteousness and truth) and find out what pleases the Lord. Have nothing to do with the fruitless deeds of darkness, but rather expose them. For it is shameful even to mention what the disobedient do in secret. But everything exposed by the light becomes visible, for it is light that makes everything visible. This is why it is said: “Wake up, O sleeper, rise from the dead, and Christ will shine on you.”

Be very careful, then, how you live—not as unwise but as wise, making the most of every opportunity, because the days are evil. Therefore do not be foolish, but understand what the Lord’s will is. Do not get drunk on wine, which leads to debauchery. Instead, be filled with the Spirit. Speak to one another with psalms, hymns and spiritual songs. Sing and make music in your heart to the Lord, always giving thanks to God the Father for everything, in the name of our Lord Jesus Christ.

Submit to one another out of reverence for Christ. (Ephesians 5:1–21 NIV)

Biblical instructions to family members in God's kingdom

Kingdom Principles for Different Roles

1. God's Instruction to Wives in His Kingdom

> Wives, submit to your husbands as to the Lord. For the husband is the head of the wife as Christ is the head of the church, his body, of which he is the Savior. Now as the church submits to Christ, so also wives should submit to their husbands in everything. (Ephesians 5:22–24 NIV)

2. God's Instructions to Husbands in His Kingdom

> Husbands, love your wives, just as Christ loved the church and gave himself up for her to make her holy, cleansing her by the washing with water through the word, and to present her to himself as a radiant church, without stain or wrinkle or any other blemish, but holy and blameless. In this same way, husbands ought to love their wives as their own bodies. He who loves his wife loves himself. After all, no one ever hated his own body, but he feeds

> and cares for it, just as Christ does the church—for we are members of his body. "For this reason a man will leave his father and mother and be united to his wife, and the two will become one flesh." This is a profound mystery—but I am talking about Christ and the church. However, each one of you also must love his wife as he loves himself, and the wife must respect her husband. (Ephesians 5:25–33 NIV)

3. God's Instructions to Children in His Kingdom

> Children, obey your parents in the Lord, for this is right. "Honor your father and mother"—which is the first commandment with a promise "that it may go well with you and that you may enjoy long life on the earth." (Ephesians 6:1–3 NIV)

4. God's Instructions to Fathers in His Kingdom

> Fathers, do not exasperate your children; instead, bring them up in the training and instruction of the Lord. (Ephesians 6:4 NIV)

Because we who are parents and a part of God's kingdom, it is our responsibility to teach children the ways of our heavenly father and the laws of his kingdom. Our opinions do not matter when it comes to a point where we have to decide the best thing to do or the best choice to make. God's word always rules, not our opinions.

5. God's Instructions to People Who Were Slaves in His Kingdom

This principle can be applied to people who are employed and have bosses.

> Slaves, obey your earthly masters with respect and fear, and with sincerity of heart, just as you would obey Christ. Obey them not only to win their favor when their eye is on you, but like slaves of Christ, doing the will of God from your heart. Serve wholeheartedly, as if you were serving the Lord, not men, because you know that the Lord will reward everyone for whatever good he does, whether he is slave or free. (Ephesians 6:5–8 NIV)

> Slavery may still exist in some countries however here in America I see a different type of slavery. Abuse is present, suffering is present and many people feel as though they are trapped in places of employment. Especially those who personal records are flawed. I have known people who have come to Bible Way jobless and we have prayed for them to find employment. These people I would see months later and they would be working and their schedules always included weekends. They would tell me how they were treated and how they would love to attend church, but couldn't get off work. There are others that have work at a job for years and were miserable and some have retired from jobs and were miserable. I see debt as a slave maker.

> The Bible teaches us in Romans to owe no man nothing. The world economic system seems to be structure to keep the majority struggling financially and reward the wealthy. Making almost impossible for the people that some call poor to ever be debt free.

Owe no man any thing, but to love one another: for he that loveth another hath fulfilled the law. (Romans 13:8`)KJV

We should work on a job as if God himself were present and watching. I don't believe that many Christians feel this way, but it is what God requires. You may not receive recognition for what you do or be treated fairly. God knows, and he will reward you for your service because you are a part of his kingdom.

Being a part of God's kingdom means we have dual citizenship, and because of this we have help from the invisible world working in the visible on our behalves. The place where you serve as an employee is only a channel for momentary provisions; it might be for a season, or it could be where you retire from. We are living in times where things are very unstable and our economy is often shaky.

In God's kingdom, there is a vast supply, and things are always stable and unchangeable. What God has established for us will last. David said in Psalm 37:25–26, "I was young and now I am old, yet I have never seen the righteous forsaken or their children begging bread. They are always generous and lend freely; their children will be blessed."

6. God's Instructions to Masters or Employers in His Kingdom

> And masters, treat your slaves in the same way. Do not threaten them, since you know that he who is both their Master and yours is in heaven, and there is no favoritism with him. (Ephesians 6:9 NIV)

Bosses who confess and profess to be children of God should treat people fairly. They should not pay one person a lower pay than someone else who is doing the same type of work. Both are living in the same system, and both need to survive.

The boss who practices this can cause one family to have a totally different espouser to life because of the difference in wages. This type of unfairness creates for a family burdens that should not exist. The only way this type of inequality in pay could exist it would have to deem so.

As a boss be fair and impartial with all who work for you, if you are an overseer of employees. God sees everything, and he will deal with each one of us on the basis of what we do (or do not do) according to his word. There is an old saying that is familiar to many of us: what we dish out will return in some form. The bible states it this way: Be not deceived; God is not mocked: for whatsoever a man soweth, that shall he also reap (Galatians 6:7KJV). It might not be identical; however, you will know the reason because of the effect it causes in your life.

7. Be Strong in the Lord

> Finally, be strong in the Lord and in his mighty power. Put on the full armor of God so that you can take your stand against the devil's schemes. (Ephesians 6:10–11 NIV)

8. Get Suited Up (Put on the Full Armor of God)

> Put on the full armor of God so that you can take your stand against the devil's schemes. For our struggle is not against flesh and blood, but against the rulers, against the authorities, against the powers of this dark world and against the spiritual forces of evil in the heavenly realms. Therefore put on the full armor of God, so that when the day of evil comes, you may be able to stand your ground, and after you have done everything, to stand. Stand firm then, with the belt of truth buckled around your waist, with the breastplate of righteousness in place, and with your feet fitted with the readiness that comes from the gospel of peace. In addition to all this, take up the shield of faith, with which you can extinguish all the flaming arrows of the evil one. Take the helmet of salvation and the sword of the Spirit, which is the word of God. And pray in the Spirit on all occasions with all kinds of prayers and requests. With this in mind, be alert and always keep on praying for all the saints. (Ephesians 6:11–18 NIV)

Conclusion

I know that some people are out there in the world living in pain and some might be on the verge of committing suicide. I also know that there are many struggling with thoughts from their past as well as those with parent issues.

I hope that some of these individuals will find this book and its message enlightening and helpful. What I have learned from the Holy Spirit and through obedience has taught me that God will take of those who trust in him. I love this simple but awesome prayer of King David found in Psalms 51:

Create in me a pure heart, O God, and renew a steadfast spirit within me. (Psalms 51:10 NIV)

This prayer and mindset will put you on the right path. My final scripture that I will share with you is from Isaiah 40:

Even youths grow tired and weary, and young men stumble and fall; but those who hope in the Lord will renew their strength. They will soar on wings like eagles; they will run and not grow weary, they will walk and not be faint. (Isaiah 40:30-31 NIV). This verse says to me that even in the prime of life a person can become tired and even though you might stumble and fall, if you trust in God and wait you will come forth like pure gold. It is my prayer that in some way, that the message and my desire to help others permeate the pages of Diagnose and Repair.

Thank you

I want to take a moment to thank my wife Paula Joyner Kirkland for her support and patience through the years of our marriage. You truly have been an inspiration and I have learned many things from you. I Thank God for being the center of our life and the glue that has held us together. It has been an Honor and blessing to grow with you these many years.

To my biological children and the children that I have helped raised your conversations and actions has taught me so much about how children view parents and how you view events in your life. This has helped me to understand more about your expectations of me as a father and has encourage me through the years to strive to be a better father. My dad was not in my life in any way and when I asked you how it feels to have a dad your answers gave me joy. For any pain or disappointments that I might have caused you because of my lack of knowledge as a dad I ask for your forgiveness.

I thank every member of Bible Way Christian Center of Pittsburg California and Bible Way Church of Abilene Texas for working with me and allowing me to serve you as you're under Shepard for the many years that I have served. To those of you who helped me with People for Improvements and the Mountain View Neighborhood Watch group in Pittsburg California you were a blessing. We fed the homeless, marched, sponsored events and protested against injustice and drugs in our city together. Thank you for your support together we made a difference in the city of Pittsburg.

To Pastor Larry Adams and members of Golden Hills community Church of Antioch California it was because of your support that we were able to complete the work needed in order for Bible Way Christian center to receive its occupancy permit from the city of Pittsburg.

You also made it possible for Bible Way in Abilene Texas, you were an answer to many years of prayer. Thank you.

To my sisters and brothers I am grateful that we are family and I love each one of you. Momma Leola and Momma Lela raised us well and I thank them for their sacrifices and the spankings and lessons that they taught us. We all have a heart that is compassionate towards others and have always been willing to help others even those who did not like us. Charline, Andrea and Shelia if I were to become ill and needed the care of an RN you three would be on the top of my list to take care of me. Not because you are family but because of the way that I have seen you care for patients. Carl and Lamar you two are some good hearted hard working men that I would want to have my back at any time. I love all of you very much. To Bishop Rob Nichols of Pater Theological Seminary, thank you for honoring my many years of service and achievements as a minister with an Honorary Doctors. A big thank you to those who helped with the ceremony. God I thank you for everything.

About the Author

Mr. Kirkland was born in 1954 and raised by his mother Leola Kirkland and grandmother Lela Duncan in the small farming town of Gunnison Mississippi, a town located in the Delta. He is the oldest of seven sibling's sisters, Charline, Johnett, Shelia and brothers, Andre, Lamar and Carl. As a minor he worked with his mother, sisters and brothers in the cotton fields, cue cumber fields and pecan orchards.

He dropped out of high school around the age of sixteen and signed up to go to the Job Corps. While he was stationed at Breckinridge Job corps center near Henderson Kentucky, Mr. Kirkland received a Breckinridge HIGH SCHOOL EQUIVALENCY CERTIFICATE on January 27, 1982. Mr. While at Breckinridge Job corps center, he was also attending classes to become a certified CARPENTER and received a DIPLOMA IN CARPENTRY on April 11, 1972. After returning home he continued his education by enrolling into COHOMA JR. COLLEGE in Clarksdale Mississippi and completed two semesters.

Mr. Kirkland accepted Jesus as his personal savior at the age of nine years old and received his LICENSE to preach on July 27, 1975 at the age of twenty one. On October 8, 1975, Mr. Kirkland was ORDAINED as a LICENSE A BAPTIST PREACHER. Mr. Kirkland joined the ARMY on November tenth nineteen seventy seven and served as a 19D10 Cavalry Scout in an Air Cavalry Unit at Ft. Ord California. He was HONORABLY discharged on February 13, 1979 due to a sustain injury while on active duty. In 1981, Mr. Kirkland enrolled into BETHANY BIBLE COLLEGE an ASSEMBLY of GOD DENOMINATION in Scotts Valley California.

Mr. Kirkland attended Bethany Bible College for three years until a much needed student aid was no longer available to help him pay for his studies.

While at Bethany Bible College MR. Kirkland had the opportunity to serve as PRESIDENT of the INTERNATIONAL TEAM MINISTRY which was composed of thirteen students from Bethany. They would travel to different towns to share the Gospel message on the streets. Once they went to San Francisco to minister to strangers on the street and this was an interesting experience. The group also were invited to different churches to participate and share in their worship services. This opportunity provided for him a new experiences, a chance to be in other denominational churches among a predominate group of Caucasian people. He had a wonderful time and felt only love in their presence. He also has had the opportunity after school to return and preach again at some of the churches that he had visited and ran some revivals because of The International Team ministry and friends at Bethany. He is thankful for the years at Bethany and friends that he met while there. It was some of those friends at Bethany from Antioch that provided him with the opportunity to visit Antioch California while he was in school.

After leaving Bethany some time in 1983, he was welcomed into the home of Arlen and Kathy Walker who had three children and they treated him as one of their own children. He looked for employment and finally signed up with the Carpenters Union in Martinez as a Journeyman Carpenter. During the next three years he would have part time jobs that barley kept him going financially. Mr. Kirkland contacted Virgie Realty Company in Oakland California that dealt with a lot of foreclosure properties to see if they had any work. They did have a job where they needed someone to go and remove the stuff that these prior owners had left behind in these foreclosed houses.

Many places were filled with garbage because people quit paying for garbage pickup and use the garage or inside of the house to store the waste. Mr. Kirkland has had many hard times in his life and has been penniless and homeless. He acknowledges that he has made many bad decisions and that he had many failures, heart aches, financial burdens and disappointments because of the decisions that he made.

He acknowledges that he has hurt people emotionally and been hurt by people emotionally, however he never purposed in his heart to hurt anyone. Many of his failures were caused because of disobedience to his parents' teachings, disobedience to God's word and the lack of knowledge, understanding and wisdom.

Around 1984 he move to Pittsburg California and in 1986 he applied for a position as a maintenance supervisor with the Housing Authority of The Contra Costa County. Mr. Kirkland had two interviews and the last of the two was with Mr. Richard Martinez. He mentioned that he remembered part of the conversation as though it was yesterday. Mr. Martinez told him that he had a number of people who had applied for this job and many of them had more experience in supervising in this capacity than he did but, (Mr. Martinez) said "I have a feeling about you that I cannot shake". His reply to Mr. Martinez, "that's God". Mr. Kirkland was hired and received at least four CERTIFICATES OF COMMENDATIONS between 1989 and 1991 for his work ethics in improving the conditions and enhancing the quality of life for the tenants of El Pueblo housing development. Mr. Kirkland attended many training seminars to better prepare him for his role as a supervisor and completed each one of them.

In 1990 he worked with other people in his neighborhood and surrounding neighborhoods to establish MOUNTAIN VIEW NEIGHBORHOOD WATCH. It was with this group that he organized meetings with the community and the Pittsburg Police Department to develop better relationships and combat drug problems. Mr. Kirkland later incorporated PFI, PPEOPLE FOR IMPROVEMENTS a nonprofit organization with a primary mission of HELPING ONE PERSON EXCELL. Through this program they offered food, clothing, tutoring for children and many other needs were met through volunteers of this organizations.

On October 15.1992 he completed a long training in San Francisco California Offered by the NATIONAL CENTER FOR HOUSING MANAGEMENT out of Washington, DC to become a CERTIFIED MANAGER OF MAINTENANCE. On December 30, 1991 he was Elected to serve as the CHARMAN OF THE CIVIC COMMITTEE FOR THE

INTER- DENOMINATIONAL MINISTERIAL ALLIANCE of Pittsburg, California. On April 14, 1998, after attending and completing the Pittsburg Police volunteer Academy class received a certificate of completion and became one of their CHAPLIANS. On June 27, 1999, he received a BACHELOR OF THEOLOGY from Sacramento Theological Seminary and Bible College, Sacramento California.

On January 1, 2012, he received a CERTIFICATE OF ACHIEVEMENT Level one from MMI, Myles Munroe International Mentoring program. Mr. Kirkland and his wife Paula Joyner-Kirkland continued studies with Dr. Myles Munroe by attending seminars in the Bahamas, purchasing his books and traveling on a trip to Israel. Lastly Mr. Kirkland received an Honorary DOCTOR OF SACRED LETTERS HONOR CAUSA, from PATER THEOLOGICAL SEMINARY, Abilene Texas by DR. R. A. Nichols.

Mr. Kirkland Has incorporated two churches on faith, Bible Way Christian Center in Pittsburg California and Bible Way Church in Abilene, Texas. He has 32 years of pastoring experience and 44 years of preaching. Mr. Kirkland states that because the churches were small in number at times he was able to get to know his fellow brothers and sisters and they taught him a lot over the years. Over the thirty plus years of pastor he met and got to know a throng of people, many who were not part of his congregation relied on his wisdom for guidance.

He is the AUTHOR of three books Enlighten, published in 2000. This books focus is on the emotional feeling associated with the caregiver of a dying person and the emotions felt after death. His second book titled LEARNING AND UNDERSTANDING HOW TO MANNAGE OUR LIIVES EFFECTIVELY WITH THE BATTLE THAT EXIST WITH IN was published in 2010. This book focus is on the many thoughts and interpretations of the thoughts that a person has associated with painful emotions of the pass attached to memories and provides other perspectives of looking at that memory.

His third book titled KNOW YOUR ENEMY AND HIS TACTICS was published on 2012. This book is focused on unveiling the camouflage of the devil his language and deceptions used on all of us and how accepting his lies and falling for his deception can mess our lives up quick.

It is from his fifty five year relationship with God, the studying of the Bible, the aid of the Holy Spirit, prayer, his formal education and experiences of Counseling over many decades and pastoring that he has drawn from to compose, publish and share his book with the world. It is what he has learned that has help him with is thinking and decision making to become a better person. Mr. Kirkland understands his relationship with GOD, the presence of the HOLY SPIRIT in his life and learning the laws and principles found in the Bible and practicing them to be most valuable. His missions and passion continues to remain the same To Offer HOPE to those who are lost and hurting and his goal is fixed on HELPING ONE PERSON EXCELL in life.

www.ingramcontent.com/pod-product-compliance
Ingram Content Group UK Ltd.
Pitfield, Milton Keynes, MK11 3LW, UK
UKHW020238250726
13967UKWH00001B/437

9 781684 707188